© 2024 by BINISH SHAH. All rights reserved.

This book, titled **"Islam and Human Rights: A Comprehensive Guide"**, along with its contents encompassing text, illustrations, images, diagrams, and other creative elements, is the exclusive property of BINISH SHAH and is safeguarded by copyright law.

BINISH SHAH asserts full ownership and retains all rights to this book. No part of this publication may be reproduced, distributed, or transmitted in any form or by any means, such as photocopying, recording, or electronic methods, without prior written consent from the copyright holder. Brief quotations in critical reviews and certain noncommercial uses permitted by copyright law are exceptions.

This copyright notice applies to all editions, formats, and translations of the book, whether in print, digital, or any other medium or technology existing now or developed in the future. Unauthorized use or infringement may result in legal action and pursuit of remedies under applicable copyright laws.

While efforts have been made to ensure accuracy and reliability, BINISH SHAH does not guarantee the completeness or suitability of the information. Readers are responsible for evaluating and using the content judiciously.

BINISH SHAH reserves the right to make changes, updates, or corrections to the book without prior notice. Inclusion of third-party materials or references does not imply endorsement or affiliation unless used under fair use principles or with proper permissions and attributions.

For permissions, inquiries, or requests regarding the book's use, please contact BINISH SHAH through official channels listed on their Amazon author page or provided email address.

This comprehensive copyright notice serves to protect BINISH SHAH's intellectual property rights, maintain content control, and inform users about associated restrictions and permissions.

Warm regards,

BINISH SHAH

ISLAM

AND

HUMAN RIGHTS

A COMPREHENSIVE GUIDE

Table of Content

Preface

Chapter 1: Introduction to Islam and Human Rights

Chapter 2: Historical Perspective

Chapter 3: Quranic Foundations

Chapter 4: Prophetic Traditions

Chapter 5: Islamic Jurisprudence

Chapter 6: Women's Rights in Islam

Chapter 7: Freedom of Religion

Chapter 8: Rights of Minorities

Chapter 9: Social Justice

Chapter 10: Environmental Rights

Chapter 11: Human Dignity

Chapter 12: Rights of the Elderly and Disabled

Chapter 13: Children's Rights

Chapter 14: Marriage and Family Rights

Chapter 15: Justice System

Chapter 16: Freedom of Expression

Chapter 17: Political Rights

Chapter 18: Economic Rights

Chapter 19: Health and Well-being

Chapter 20: Education Rights

Chapter 21: Refugees and Migration

Chapter 22: Conflict Resolution

Chapter 23: International Relations

Chapter 24: Humanitarian Aid and Charity

Chapter 25: Ethics in Business and Commerce

Chapter 26: Cultural Rights

Chapter 27: Technology and Innovation

Chapter 28: Animal Rights

Chapter 29: Social Welfare and Safety Nets

Chapter 30: The Future of Human Rights in Islam

Chapter 31: Case Studies

Chapter 32: Comparative Perspectives

Chapter 33: Human Rights Advocacy

Chapter 34: Legal Frameworks

Chapter 35: Education and Awareness

Chapter 36: Grassroots Movements

Chapter 37: International Cooperation

Chapter 38: Challenges and Controversies

Chapter 39: Human Rights and Development

Chapter 40: Gender Equality

Chapter 41: Youth and Human Rights

Chapter 42: Media and Communication

Chapter 43: Religious Freedom

Chapter 44: Accountability and Justice

Chapter 45: Peacebuilding and Reconciliation

Chapter 46: Ethics of War

Chapter 47: Governance and Human Rights

Chapter 48: Legal Protections

Chapter 49: Social Movements and Change (Continued)

Chapter 50: Conclusion

Preface

In recent years, the intersection of Islam and human rights has been a topic of increasing importance and relevance. As the global community grapples with issues of human rights violations and abuses, particularly in regions with significant Muslim populations, there is a growing need to understand the relationship between Islamic teachings and the protection and promotion of human rights.

This book, "Islam and Human Rights: A Comprehensive Guide," seeks to provide readers with a thorough and balanced exploration of this complex and multifaceted relationship. Drawing on a wide range of sources, including the Quran, Hadith, Islamic jurisprudence, and historical and contemporary examples, this book aims to provide a comprehensive overview of how Islam views and addresses human rights issues.

The book is divided into fifty chapters, each focusing on a different aspect of the relationship between Islam and human rights. It begins with an introduction to the concept of human rights in Islam, exploring the foundational principles and values that underpin Islamic teachings on human rights. Subsequent chapters delve into specific human rights issues, such as women's rights, freedom of religion, and the rights of minorities, providing readers with a detailed understanding of Islamic perspectives on these topics.

Throughout the book, readers will encounter a range of perspectives and opinions, reflecting the diversity of thought within the Islamic tradition. The goal is not to present a monolithic view of Islam and human rights, but rather to encourage readers to engage critically with the material and form their own informed opinions.

It is my hope that this book will serve as a valuable resource for scholars, students, policymakers, and anyone interested in deepening their understanding of the relationship between Islam and human rights. By fostering dialogue and understanding, we can work towards a more just and inclusive world for all.

Chapter 1: Introduction to Islam and Human Rights

A: Overview of the Relationship between Islam and Human Rights

Islam, as a comprehensive way of life, places a strong emphasis on the rights of individuals and communities. The relationship between Islam and human rights is rooted in the belief that every human being is inherently dignified and possesses certain rights that must be respected and protected. Islamic teachings provide a framework for understanding and promoting human rights, encompassing principles of justice, equality, compassion, and respect for the dignity of all individuals.

Islam's view of human rights is based on the concept of "fitrah," or the innate nature of human beings, which is considered pure and inclined towards goodness. This concept forms the foundation for the rights and responsibilities outlined in Islamic teachings. The Quran, the holy book of Islam, and the teachings of the Prophet Muhammad provide guidance on the rights of individuals, including the right to life, freedom, and dignity.

Islamic teachings also emphasize the importance of social justice and the equitable distribution of resources. The concept of "zakat," or obligatory charity, highlights the responsibility of individuals and society to care for the less fortunate and ensure their basic needs are met.

B: Importance of Human Rights in Islamic Teachings

Human rights are deeply ingrained in Islamic teachings and are considered essential for the well-being of individuals and society as a whole. Islam recognizes the inherent dignity of every human being, regardless of race, religion, or background, and emphasizes the importance of treating others with respect and compassion.

Islamic teachings stress the importance of justice and fairness in all aspects of life. The Quran explicitly states, "O you who have believed, be persistently standing firm in justice, witnesses for Allah, even if it be against yourselves or parents and relatives" (Quran 4:135). This verse highlights the obligation to uphold justice, even if it goes against one's own interests.

Furthermore, Islam emphasizes the rights of marginalized groups, including women, children, and the elderly. Islamic teachings promote gender equality, protect the rights of children, and emphasize the importance of caring for the elderly and disabled.

In conclusion, Islam places a strong emphasis on human rights, viewing them as essential for a just and compassionate society. The teachings of Islam provide a comprehensive framework for understanding and promoting human rights, encompassing principles of justice, equality, and compassion for all individuals.

Chapter 2: Historical Perspective

A: History of Human Rights in Islamic Societies

Islamic societies have a long history of respecting and upholding human rights, dating back to the early days of Islam. One of the key principles of Islamic governance is the protection of the rights of all individuals, regardless of their background or beliefs. This principle is enshrined in the Quran and the teachings of the Prophet Muhammad, who emphasized the importance of justice, compassion, and equality.

During the early Islamic period, Muslim rulers implemented laws and policies that protected the rights of minorities, ensured the fair treatment of prisoners of war, and promoted social justice. Islamic societies also developed advanced legal systems that guaranteed the rights of individuals, including the right to a fair trial and protection from unjust treatment.

One of the most notable examples of human rights in Islamic societies is the Charter of Medina, which was drafted by the Prophet Muhammad shortly after his arrival in the city of Medina. This charter established the rights of all citizens, regardless of their religious beliefs, and laid the foundation for a pluralistic and inclusive society.

Throughout history, Islamic societies have continued to uphold the principles of human rights, even in the face of political turmoil and external pressures. Today, many Islamic countries are signatories to international human rights treaties and have implemented laws and policies to protect the rights of their citizens.

B: Influence of Islamic Principles on Early Human Rights Movements

Islamic principles have had a significant influence on early human rights movements, particularly in the Middle East and North Africa. The teachings of Islam, which emphasize the importance of justice, equality, and compassion, provided a moral and ethical framework for these movements.

One of the key figures in the early human rights movements influenced by Islamic principles was Jamal al-Din al-Afghani, an Islamic scholar and political activist who advocated for social justice and political reform in the Muslim world. Al-Afghani's teachings emphasized the importance of upholding the rights of individuals and promoting a just and equitable society.

Another influential figure was Muhammad Abduh, an Egyptian Islamic scholar who played a key role in the reform of Islamic thought in the late 19th and early 20th centuries. Abduh argued for a reinterpretation of Islamic teachings to promote social justice, equality, and human rights.

The influence of Islamic principles on early human rights movements can also be seen in the development of human rights treaties and declarations in the Muslim world. Many of these documents draw on Islamic teachings to justify the protection of human rights and promote social justice.

Overall, the historical perspective of human rights in Islamic societies highlights the importance of Islamic principles in promoting a just and compassionate society. Islamic teachings have had a profound influence on early human rights movements, shaping the development of human rights principles in the Muslim world.

Chapter 3: Quranic Foundations

A: Examination of Key Quranic Verses Related to Human Rights

The Quran, as the holy book of Islam, contains numerous verses that emphasize the importance of human rights and outline the rights and responsibilities of individuals. These verses serve as the foundation for Islamic teachings on human rights and provide guidance on how individuals should interact with one another.

One of the key verses related to human rights in the Quran is Surah Al-Ma'idah, verse 8, which states, "O you who have believed, be persistently standing firm for Allah, witnesses in justice, and do not let the hatred of a people prevent you from being just. Be just; that is nearer to righteousness. And fear Allah; indeed, Allah is Acquainted with what you do." This verse emphasizes the importance of justice and fairness in all aspects of life and calls on believers to uphold these principles, even in the face of adversity.

Another important verse is Surah Al-Hujurat, verse 13, which states, "O mankind, indeed We have created you from male and female and made you peoples and tribes that you may know one another. Indeed, the most noble of you in the sight of Allah is the most righteous of you. Indeed, Allah is Knowing and Acquainted." This verse highlights the equality of all individuals in the eyes of Allah and emphasizes the importance of treating others with respect and compassion, regardless of their background or beliefs.

B: Principles of Justice, Equality, and Compassion in the Quran

The Quran contains numerous principles that emphasize the importance of justice, equality, and compassion in Islamic teachings. These principles serve as the foundation for human rights in Islam and provide a moral and ethical framework for how individuals should behave towards one another.

One of the key principles is the concept of 'Adl, or justice, which is mentioned numerous times in the Quran. For example, Surah An-Nisa, verse 135, states, "O you who have believed, be persistently standing firm in justice, witnesses for Allah, even if it be against yourselves or parents and relatives. Whether one is rich or poor, Allah is more worthy of both. So follow not [personal] inclination, lest you not be just. And if you distort [your testimony] or refuse [to give it], then indeed Allah is ever, with what you do, Acquainted."

Another important principle is the concept of equality, which is emphasized in many verses of the Quran. Surah Al-Hujurat, verse 13, mentioned earlier, highlights the equality of all individuals in the sight of Allah, regardless of their background or beliefs.

Compassion is also a key principle in the Quran, with numerous verses calling on believers to show compassion towards one another. Surah At-Tawbah, verse 128, states, "There has certainly come to you a Messenger from among yourselves. Grievous to him is what you suffer; [he is]

concerned over you and to the believers is kind and merciful."

Overall, the Quranic foundations of human rights in Islam emphasize the importance of justice, equality, and compassion in all aspects of life. These principles serve as a guide for believers on how to interact with one another and promote a just and equitable society.

Chapter 4: Prophetic Traditions

A: Hadiths and Sayings of the Prophet Muhammad Related to Human Rights

The Hadiths, which are collections of sayings and actions of the Prophet Muhammad, provide further guidance on human rights in Islam. These teachings complement the Quranic principles and offer practical examples of how to uphold human rights in everyday life.

One of the key Hadiths related to human rights is the Prophet's statement, "None of you truly believes until he loves for his brother what he loves for himself." This Hadith emphasizes the importance of empathy and compassion towards others, highlighting the golden rule of treating others as you would like to be treated.

Another important Hadith is the Prophet's statement, "The best among you are those who are best to their wives." This Hadith underscores the importance of respecting women's rights and treating them with kindness and compassion.

Additionally, the Prophet Muhammad emphasized the rights of neighbors in several Hadiths, stating, "Whoever believes in Allah and the Last Day should not harm his neighbor." This Hadith highlights the importance of being considerate and helpful to neighbors, regardless of their background or beliefs.

B: Examples of the Prophet's Teachings on Social Justice and Equality

The Prophet Muhammad's teachings on social justice and equality are exemplified in his actions and sayings. He advocated for the fair treatment of all individuals, regardless of their social status or background, and emphasized the importance of justice and compassion in society.

One of the key examples of the Prophet's teachings on social justice is his establishment of the Constitution of Medina, which laid the foundation for a pluralistic and inclusive society. This document guaranteed the rights of all citizens, regardless of their religious beliefs, and promoted social harmony and cooperation among different communities.

The Prophet Muhammad also practiced social justice in his daily life, often advocating for the rights of the poor and marginalized. He encouraged his followers to give to charity and support those in need, highlighting the importance of caring for the less fortunate in society.

Overall, the Prophet Muhammad's teachings on social justice and equality serve as a timeless example for Muslims on how to uphold human rights and promote a just and compassionate society. His actions and sayings continue to inspire Muslims around the world to strive for justice, equality, and compassion in all aspects of life.

Chapter 5: Islamic Jurisprudence

A: Overview of Islamic Law (Sharia) and its Relevance to Human Rights

Islamic jurisprudence, known as Sharia, is derived from the Quran and the Hadiths, as well as scholarly consensus and analogy. Sharia provides a comprehensive legal framework that covers all aspects of life, including personal conduct, family matters, economics, and governance. In the context of human rights, Sharia offers principles and guidelines that emphasize justice, equality, and compassion.

One of the key principles of Sharia relevant to human rights is the concept of Maslaha, or the common good. Sharia recognizes the importance of promoting the well-being of society as a whole and considers it a fundamental objective of Islamic law. This principle underpins many aspects of human rights in Islamic jurisprudence, such as the protection of life, property, and dignity.

Sharia also emphasizes the importance of justice in all legal matters. The Quran states, "O you who have believed, be persistently standing firm in justice, witnesses for Allah, even if it be against yourselves or parents and relatives" (Quran 4:135). This verse highlights the obligation to uphold justice, even if it goes against one's own interests, which is a fundamental principle of human rights.

Furthermore, Sharia recognizes the rights of individuals to freedom of religion and belief, as long as it does not harm others or disrupt public order. This principle aligns with the concept of freedom of religion in international human rights law.

B: Analysis of How Islamic Jurisprudence Addresses Contemporary Human Rights Issues

Islamic jurisprudence provides guidance on contemporary human rights issues, addressing them through the lens of Islamic principles and values. For example, in the context of women's rights, Sharia emphasizes the importance of gender equality and the protection of women's rights in areas such as marriage, divorce, and inheritance. While there are differences of interpretation among scholars, many Islamic countries have implemented laws and policies that protect women's rights based on Islamic teachings.

In the area of criminal justice, Sharia emphasizes the importance of due process and the rights of the accused. Islamic jurisprudence prohibits the use of torture and emphasizes the presumption of innocence until proven guilty. However, the implementation of these principles varies among Islamic countries, with some facing criticism for human rights abuses in their legal systems.

In conclusion, Islamic jurisprudence provides a framework for addressing contemporary human rights issues, drawing on Islamic principles of justice, equality, and compassion. While there are differences of interpretation among scholars and challenges in implementation, Sharia offers valuable insights into how Islamic teachings can inform discussions on human rights in the modern world.

Chapter 6: Women's Rights in Islam

A: Rights and Status of Women in Islam

Islam recognizes the rights and status of women as equal to that of men, emphasizing their dignity and worth as individuals. Islamic teachings provide guidance on women's rights in various aspects of life, including education, work, marriage, and inheritance.

In terms of education, Islam emphasizes the importance of seeking knowledge for both men and women. The Prophet Muhammad said, "Seeking knowledge is obligatory for every Muslim." This includes religious and worldly knowledge, highlighting the importance of education for women.

In the context of work, Islam allows women to engage in business and earn their own income. The Quran states, "And their Lord has accepted of them, and answered them: 'Never will I suffer to be lost the work of any of you, be he male or female: You are members, one of another...'" (Quran 3:195). This verse emphasizes the equal worth of men and women in the eyes of Allah and highlights the importance of women's contributions to society.

In terms of marriage, Islam grants women the right to choose their spouses and prohibits forced marriage. The Quran states, "And among His Signs is this, that He created for you mates from among yourselves, that you may dwell in tranquility with them, and He has put love and mercy between your (hearts): verily in that are Signs for those who reflect" (Quran 30:21). This verse emphasizes the importance of mutual love and respect in marriage, highlighting the rights of women to choose their partners and be treated with kindness and compassion.

Regarding inheritance, Islamic law guarantees women the right to inherit from their parents, spouses, and other relatives. The Quran states, "For men is a share of what the parents and close relatives leave, and for women is a share of what the parents and close relatives leave, be it little or much - an obligatory share" (Quran 4:7). This verse ensures that women receive a fair share of inheritance, regardless of societal norms or customs.

B: Misconceptions and Realities about Women's Rights in Islamic Teachings

There are many misconceptions about women's rights in Islam, often stemming from cultural practices or misinterpretations of Islamic teachings. One common misconception is that Islam oppresses women and denies them basic rights. In reality, Islam grants women rights and protections that were revolutionary at the time of revelation, such as the right to own property, seek divorce, and participate in public life.

Another misconception is that women are considered inferior to men in Islam. In reality, Islam emphasizes the equal worth of men and women in the eyes of Allah. The Quran states, "Whoever does righteousness, whether male or female, while he is a believer - We will surely cause him to live a good life, and We will surely give them their reward [in the Hereafter] according to the best of what they used to do" (Quran 16:97). This verse highlights that both men and women are equal in their ability to earn rewards from Allah through righteous deeds.

Overall, Islam recognizes and protects the rights of women, emphasizing their dignity, worth, and equality with men. While there may be differences in the interpretation and implementation of these rights, the core teachings of Islam affirm the importance of upholding women's rights and treating them with respect and dignity.

Chapter 7: Freedom of Religion

A: Islamic Perspective on Freedom of Religion and Belief

Islam emphasizes the freedom of religion and belief as a fundamental human right. The Quran states, "There shall be no compulsion in [acceptance of] the religion. The right course has become clear from the wrong" (Quran 2:256). This verse underscores the principle that individuals should not be forced to adhere to a particular religion, and that the truth should be made clear through peaceful means.

Islamic teachings also emphasize the importance of respecting the beliefs of others. The Quran states, "And do not insult those they invoke other than Allah, lest they insult Allah in enmity without knowledge. Thus We have made pleasing to every community their deeds. Then to their Lord is their return, and He will inform them about what they used to do" (Quran 6:108). This verse highlights the importance of respecting the religious beliefs of others, even if they differ from one's own.

Furthermore, Islamic history is replete with examples of religious tolerance and coexistence. During the early Islamic period, Muslim rulers granted religious minorities, such as Christians and Jews, the right to practice their faiths and maintain their religious institutions. This spirit of tolerance was exemplified in the Covenant of Medina, which guaranteed the rights of all citizens, regardless of their religious beliefs.

B: Case Studies of Religious Tolerance in Islamic History

One of the most famous examples of religious tolerance in Islamic history is the reign of the Abbasid Caliphate in Baghdad. Under Abbasid rule, Baghdad became a center of learning and culture, where scholars from different religious backgrounds, including Muslims, Christians, and Jews, coexisted and contributed to the intellectual and scientific advancement of the Islamic world.

Another example is the Umayyad Caliphate in Spain, where Muslims, Christians, and Jews lived together in relative harmony for centuries. This period, known as the "Golden Age of Al-Andalus," was marked by religious tolerance and cultural flourishing, with Muslims, Christians, and Jews making significant contributions to art, science, and philosophy.

In conclusion, Islam emphasizes the freedom of religion and belief as a fundamental human right. Islamic teachings promote religious tolerance and respect for the beliefs of others, and Islamic history offers numerous examples of religious coexistence and harmony.

Chapter 8: Rights of Minorities

A: Islamic Teachings on the Rights of Religious and Ethnic Minorities

Islam places a strong emphasis on the rights of religious and ethnic minorities, emphasizing the importance of treating them with fairness, compassion, and respect. The Quran states, "And do not let the hatred of a people for having obstructed you from the Sacred Mosque lead you to transgress. And cooperate in righteousness and piety, but do not cooperate in sin and aggression. And fear Allah; indeed, Allah is severe in penalty" (Quran 5:2). This verse highlights the importance of cooperating with others, regardless of their beliefs or background, and emphasizes the importance of treating them with kindness and fairness.

Islamic teachings also emphasize the importance of protecting the rights of minorities to practice their religion freely. The Quran states, "To you be your religion, and to me be my religion" (Quran 109:6), highlighting the principle of religious freedom and tolerance in Islam. This verse underscores the importance of respecting the beliefs of others and allowing them to practice their faith without fear of persecution.

B: Examples of Minority Rights in Islamic Societies

Throughout history, Islamic societies have implemented laws and policies that protect the rights of religious and ethnic minorities. One example is the Pact of Umar, a treaty that was granted by the second Caliph, Umar ibn al-Khattab, to the Christian community of Jerusalem. This treaty guaranteed the rights of Christians to practice their faith freely and maintain their religious institutions, while also ensuring their protection and security.

Another example is the Ottoman Empire, which was known for its policy of religious tolerance and pluralism. Under Ottoman rule, religious and ethnic minorities were granted the right to practice their faiths and maintain their cultural traditions. The millet system, which allowed each religious community to govern its own affairs, is a testament to the Ottoman Empire's commitment to minority rights.

In modern times, many Islamic countries have implemented laws and policies that protect the rights of minorities. For example, countries like Malaysia and Indonesia have laws that guarantee the rights of religious minorities to practice their faith freely and maintain their religious institutions.

Overall, Islamic teachings emphasize the importance of protecting the rights of religious and ethnic minorities. Throughout history, Islamic societies have implemented laws and policies that reflect these teachings, ensuring that minorities are treated with fairness, compassion, and respect.

Chapter 9: Social Justice

A: Islamic Principles of Social Justice and Economic Equality

Islam places a strong emphasis on social justice and economic equality, emphasizing the importance of caring for the less fortunate and ensuring that wealth is distributed fairly among all members of society. Islamic teachings promote principles of compassion, fairness, and generosity, which form the basis of social justice in Islam.

One of the key principles of social justice in Islam is the concept of "Adl," or justice. The Quran emphasizes the importance of justice in all aspects of life, stating, "O you who have believed, be persistently standing firm in justice, witnesses for Allah, even if it be against yourselves or parents and relatives. Whether one is rich or poor, Allah is more worthy of both. So follow not [personal] inclination, lest you not be just. And if you distort [your testimony] or refuse [to give it], then indeed Allah is ever, with what you do, Acquainted" (Quran 4:135). This verse highlights the obligation to uphold justice, even if it goes against one's own interests, and emphasizes the importance of treating all individuals fairly and impartially.

Another key principle is the concept of "Ihsan," or excellence in behavior. The Prophet Muhammad emphasized the importance of treating others with kindness and compassion, stating, "None of you truly believes until he loves for his brother what he loves for himself" (Sahih Bukhari). This Hadith highlights the importance of empathy and compassion towards others, regardless of their social status or background.

B: Zakat (Charity) and its Role in Addressing Poverty and Inequality

Zakat, or obligatory charity, is one of the five pillars of Islam and plays a crucial role in addressing poverty and inequality in Islamic societies. Zakat is a form of wealth redistribution that requires Muslims to give a portion of their wealth to those in need, including the poor, needy, and disadvantaged.

The Quran states, "And establish prayer and give zakat, and whatever good you put forward for yourselves - you will find it with Allah. Indeed, Allah of what you do, is Seeing" (Quran 2:110). This verse highlights the importance of zakat as a means of purifying one's wealth and seeking the pleasure of Allah.

Zakat is typically calculated as 2.5% of a Muslim's wealth and assets, including savings, investments, and property. This wealth is distributed to those in need through various channels, such as charitable organizations, mosques, and local community initiatives.

Zakat plays a crucial role in addressing poverty and inequality by providing a safety net for those in need and ensuring that wealth is distributed fairly among all members of society. By fulfilling the obligation of zakat, Muslims contribute to the welfare of their communities and uphold the principles of social justice and economic equality in Islam.

Chapter 10: Environmental Rights

A: Islamic Teachings on Environmental Conservation and Sustainability

Islam places a strong emphasis on environmental conservation and sustainability, emphasizing the importance of preserving the natural world for future generations. Islamic teachings promote principles of stewardship, moderation, and respect for the environment, which form the basis of environmental rights in Islam.

One of the key teachings of Islam regarding the environment is the concept of "Khalifa," or stewardship. The Quran states, "It is He who has made you successors (Khalifa) upon the Earth..." (Quran 35:39). This verse highlights the responsibility of human beings to act as stewards of the Earth, caring for its resources and ensuring its preservation for future generations.

Another key teaching is the concept of "Hima," or protected zones. The Prophet Muhammad established the concept of Hima, which designated certain areas as protected zones where hunting and deforestation were prohibited. This concept reflects the importance of preserving natural habitats and biodiversity in Islam.

B: Importance of Protecting the Environment in Islamic Ethics

In addition to specific teachings on environmental conservation, Islam emphasizes the importance of protecting the environment as a moral and ethical duty. The Quran states, "And do not commit abuse on the Earth, spreading corruption" (Quran 2:60). This verse highlights the prohibition of wastefulness and destruction of natural resources, emphasizing the importance of preserving the Earth's ecosystems.

Islamic ethics also emphasize the principle of "Ihsan," or excellence in behavior. The Prophet Muhammad emphasized the importance of treating the environment with kindness and respect, stating, "If a Muslim plants a tree or sows seeds, and then a bird, or a person, or an animal eats from it, it is regarded as a charitable gift (Sadaqah) for him" (Sahih Bukhari). This Hadith highlights the importance of environmental stewardship and the rewards associated with caring for the environment.

Overall, Islam emphasizes the importance of environmental conservation and sustainability, promoting principles of stewardship, moderation, and respect for the environment. By upholding these principles, Muslims contribute to the preservation of the natural world and fulfill their ethical and moral obligations as stewards of the Earth.

Chapter 11: Human Dignity

A: Concept of Human Dignity in Islam

In Islam, human dignity is a fundamental principle that underpins all aspects of human rights and social interactions. Islam teaches that every human being is created with dignity and deserves to be treated with respect and compassion.

One of the key teachings of Islam regarding human dignity is the concept of "Honouring the Children of Adam." The Quran states, "We have certainly honored the children of Adam and carried them on the land and sea and provided for them of the good things and preferred them over much of what We have created, with [definite] preference" (Quran 17:70). This verse highlights the inherent dignity of all human beings, regardless of their background or beliefs.

Islam also emphasizes the importance of treating others with kindness and respect, regardless of their social status or background. The Prophet Muhammad said, "Whoever does not show mercy to the people, Allah will not show mercy to him" (Sahih Bukhari). This Hadith emphasizes the importance of compassion and empathy towards others, highlighting the value of human dignity in Islamic teachings.

B: Importance of Respecting Human Dignity in Islamic Ethics

Respecting human dignity is central to Islamic ethics, which emphasize the importance of treating others with respect, fairness, and compassion. Islam teaches that all human beings are equal in the sight of Allah and should be treated as such.

One of the key principles of Islamic ethics is the concept of "Ihsan," or excellence in behavior. The Prophet Muhammad emphasized the importance of treating others with kindness and respect, stating, "Do not belittle any good deed, even if it is just greeting your brother with a cheerful face" (Sahih Muslim). This Hadith highlights the importance of small acts of kindness and respect in Islamic ethics, emphasizing the value of human dignity.

Overall, Islam places a strong emphasis on human dignity and teaches that every human being deserves to be treated with respect, compassion, and kindness. By upholding these principles, Muslims contribute to the promotion of a just and compassionate society, where all individuals are valued and respected.

Chapter 12: Rights of the Elderly and Disabled

A: Islamic Teachings on Caring for the Elderly and Disabled

Islam emphasizes the importance of caring for the elderly and disabled, emphasizing the value and dignity of every individual regardless of age or ability. Islamic teachings promote compassion, respect, and support for the elderly and disabled, highlighting their rights to care and dignity.

One of the key teachings of Islam regarding the elderly is the concept of "Sila Rahmi," or maintaining ties with kinship. The Quran states, "And worship Allah and associate nothing with Him, and to parents do good, and to relatives, orphans, the needy, the near neighbor, the neighbor farther away, the companion at your side, the traveler, and those whom your right hands possess. Indeed, Allah does not like those who are self-deluding and boastful" (Quran 4:36). This verse emphasizes the importance of caring for parents and relatives, including the elderly, and treating them with kindness and respect.

Islam also emphasizes the importance of caring for the disabled and ensuring their inclusion in society. The Prophet Muhammad said, "He who does not show mercy to our young ones and does not realize the rights of our elderly is not one of us" (Sunan Abi Dawud). This Hadith highlights the importance of showing compassion and support for the elderly and disabled, emphasizing their rights to care and dignity.

B: Examples of Support for the Elderly and Disabled in Islamic Societies

Islamic societies have a long history of supporting the elderly and disabled, providing care and assistance to those in need. In many Islamic countries, there are traditions of extended families living together, which helps to ensure that the elderly and disabled are cared for within the family unit.

Islamic societies also have a tradition of charitable giving, including supporting the elderly and disabled. Zakat, or obligatory charity, is one of the five pillars of Islam and requires Muslims to give a portion of their wealth to those in need, including the elderly and disabled.

Furthermore, many Islamic countries have implemented social welfare programs to support the elderly and disabled. These programs provide financial assistance, healthcare, and other services to ensure that the needs of the elderly and disabled are met.

Overall, Islam emphasizes the importance of caring for the elderly and disabled, highlighting their rights to care and dignity. Islamic societies have a long history of supporting the elderly and disabled, providing care and assistance to ensure their well-being and inclusion in society.

Chapter 13: Children's Rights

A: Rights of Children in Islam

Islam places a strong emphasis on the rights of children, recognizing them as vulnerable members of society who deserve protection, care, and guidance. Islamic teachings promote the well-being and rights of children, emphasizing their rights to love, protection, education, and health care.

One of the key teachings of Islam regarding children is the concept of "Sadaqah Jariyah," or continuous charity. The Prophet Muhammad said, "When a person dies, his deeds come to an end except for three: Sadaqah Jariyah (a continuous charity), or knowledge from which benefit is gained, or a righteous child who prays for him" (Sahih Muslim). This Hadith highlights the importance of raising righteous and virtuous children, who will continue to benefit society even after their parents have passed away.

Islam also emphasizes the importance of providing for the material and emotional needs of children. The Quran states, "And those who, when they spend, do so not excessively or sparingly but are ever, between that, [justly] moderate" (Quran 25:67). This verse highlights the importance of providing for children's needs in a balanced and moderate manner, ensuring that they are not deprived or neglected.

B: Importance of Protecting Children from Harm and Exploitation

Islam emphasizes the importance of protecting children from harm and exploitation, highlighting their vulnerability and the need for special care and protection. The Prophet

Muhammad said, "Whoever does not show mercy to our young ones and does not realize the rights of our elderly is not one of us" (Sunan Abi Dawud). This Hadith emphasizes the importance of showing compassion and care for children, ensuring that their rights are protected and their well-being is ensured.

Furthermore, Islam prohibits the abuse and exploitation of children, emphasizing the need to protect them from harm. The Quran states, "And do not kill your children for fear of poverty. We provide for them and for you. Indeed, their killing is a great sin" (Quran 17:31). This verse highlights the prohibition of harming or neglecting children, emphasizing the importance of their protection and well-being.

Overall, Islam places a strong emphasis on the rights of children, recognizing them as vulnerable members of society who deserve protection, care, and guidance. By upholding these principles, Muslims contribute to the well-being and rights of children, ensuring that they are protected from harm and exploitation.

Chapter 14: Marriage and Family Rights

A: Islamic Teachings on Marriage, Family, and Parenting

Islam places a strong emphasis on the importance of marriage, family, and parenting, recognizing these institutions as fundamental to a healthy and stable society. Islamic teachings provide guidance on marriage, family life, and parenting, emphasizing the rights and responsibilities of individuals within the family unit.

Marriage in Islam is considered a sacred bond between a man and a woman, based on mutual love, respect, and understanding. The Quran states, "And of His signs is that He created for you from yourselves mates that you may find tranquility in them; and He placed between you affection and mercy. Indeed in that are signs for a people who give thought" (Quran 30:21). This verse highlights the purpose of marriage in Islam, which is to find tranquility, affection, and mercy in the relationship.

Islamic teachings also emphasize the importance of family life and parenting. The Quran instructs parents to be kind and just towards their children, stating, "And lower to them the wing of humility out of mercy and say, 'My Lord, have mercy upon them as they brought me up [when I was] small'" (Quran 17:24). This verse highlights the importance of showing kindness, mercy, and respect towards children, recognizing the role of parents in nurturing and raising them.

B: Rights and Responsibilities within the Family Unit in Islam

Islam emphasizes the rights and responsibilities of individuals within the family unit, outlining the roles of husbands, wives, parents, and children. For example, husbands are required to provide for their wives and families, while wives are required to obey their husbands and maintain the household. The Quran states, "Men are in charge of women by [right of] what Allah has given one over the other and what they spend [for maintenance] from their wealth. So righteous women are devoutly obedient, guarding in [the husband's] absence what Allah would have them guard" (Quran 4:34).

Similarly, parents are responsible for the upbringing and well-being of their children, while children are required to respect and obey their parents. The Quran states, "And your Lord has decreed that you not worship except Him, and to parents, good treatment. Whether one or both of them reach old age [while] with you, say not to them [so much as], 'uff,' and do not repel them but speak to them a noble word" (Quran 17:23).

Overall, Islam emphasizes the importance of marriage, family, and parenting, providing guidance on the rights and responsibilities of individuals within the family unit. By upholding these principles, Muslims contribute to the well-being and stability of the family unit, which is considered the cornerstone of a healthy society.

Chapter 15: Justice System

A: Islamic Principles of Justice and Fairness in Legal Systems

Islam places a strong emphasis on justice and fairness in legal systems, emphasizing the importance of upholding the rights of individuals and ensuring that they are treated with equity and impartiality. Islamic teachings provide guidance on the principles of justice and fairness, which form the basis of legal systems in Islamic societies.

One of the key principles of justice in Islam is the concept of "Qist," or fairness. The Quran states, "O you who have believed, be persistently standing firm in justice, witnesses for Allah, even if it be against yourselves or parents and relatives. Whether one is rich or poor, Allah is more worthy of both. So follow not [personal] inclination, lest you not be just. And if you distort [your testimony] or refuse [to give it], then indeed Allah is ever, with what you do, Acquainted" (Quran 4:135). This verse emphasizes the importance of being fair and just in all legal matters, regardless of personal interests or biases.

Islam also emphasizes the importance of equality before the law. The Quran states, "And when you testify, be just, even if [it concerns] a near relative. And the covenant of Allah fulfill. This has He instructed you that you may remember" (Quran 6:152). This verse highlights the importance of treating all individuals equally under the law, ensuring that justice is applied impartially and without discrimination.

B: Role of Judges and Courts in Upholding Human Rights in Islamic Law

In Islamic law, judges and courts play a crucial role in upholding human rights and ensuring that justice is served. Islamic legal systems are based on the principles of Sharia, which provide guidelines for judges to ensure that legal decisions are fair, equitable, and in accordance with Islamic teachings.

One of the key roles of judges in Islamic law is to ensure that all parties are treated fairly and that their rights are protected. The Prophet Muhammad said, "The judges are of three types, one of whom will go to Paradise and two to Hell. The one who will go to Paradise is a man who knows what is right and gives judgment accordingly" (Sahih Bukhari). This Hadith emphasizes the importance of judges being knowledgeable and fair in their decisions, ensuring that justice is served.

Furthermore, Islamic law emphasizes the importance of ensuring that legal proceedings are conducted in a transparent and accountable manner. The Quran states, "And do not consume one another's wealth unjustly or send it [in bribery] to the rulers in order that [they might aid] you [to] consume a portion of the wealth of the people in sin, while you know [it is unlawful]" (Quran 2:188). This verse highlights the prohibition of corruption and bribery in legal proceedings, emphasizing the importance of upholding justice and fairness in all legal matters.

Overall, Islamic legal systems emphasize the importance of justice, fairness, and accountability in upholding human rights. Judges and courts play a crucial role in ensuring that these principles are upheld, ensuring that justice is served and human rights are protected in Islamic societies.

Chapter 16: Freedom of Expression

A: Islamic Perspective on Freedom of Speech and Expression

Islam recognizes the importance of freedom of speech and expression as a fundamental human right, allowing individuals to express their thoughts, ideas, and opinions freely. Islamic teachings emphasize the importance of seeking knowledge, exchanging ideas, and engaging in constructive dialogue.

One of the key teachings of Islam regarding freedom of expression is the concept of "Ijtihad," or independent reasoning. Islam encourages individuals to use their intellect and reasoning to understand and interpret religious teachings, allowing for diverse opinions and interpretations. The Quran states, "So ask the people of the message if you do not know" (Quran 16:43), emphasizing the importance of seeking knowledge and consulting with others to gain a deeper understanding of religious teachings.

Islam also emphasizes the importance of freedom of expression in matters of public interest. The Prophet Muhammad said, "The best jihad is a word of truth in front of a tyrant ruler" (Sunan Abi Dawud). This Hadith highlights the importance of speaking out against injustice and oppression, even in the face of adversity.

B: Limits and Responsibilities Associated with Freedom of Expression in Islam

While Islam recognizes the importance of freedom of expression, it also sets limits and responsibilities to ensure that it is exercised responsibly and in a manner that does not harm others or violate Islamic principles. Islam prohibits speech that incites hatred, violence, or division among people. The Quran states, "And do not insult those they invoke other than Allah, lest they insult Allah in enmity without knowledge. Thus We have made pleasing to every community their deeds. Then to their Lord is their return, and He will inform them about what they used to do" (Quran 6:108).

Furthermore, Islam emphasizes the importance of speaking the truth and avoiding falsehood. The Prophet Muhammad said, "Be truthful, for indeed truthfulness leads to righteousness, and righteousness leads to Paradise. And a man keeps on telling the truth until he is written with Allah as a truthful person" (Sahih Bukhari). This Hadith highlights the importance of honesty and integrity in speech, emphasizing the responsibility of individuals to speak the truth and avoid spreading falsehoods.

Overall, Islam recognizes the importance of freedom of expression as a fundamental human right, allowing individuals to express their thoughts and ideas freely. However, Islam also sets limits and responsibilities to ensure that freedom of expression is exercised responsibly and in accordance with Islamic principles, emphasizing the importance of speaking the truth and avoiding speech that incites hatred or violence.

Chapter 17: Political Rights

A: Islamic Teachings on Governance, Leadership, and Political Participation

Islam provides guidance on governance, leadership, and political participation, emphasizing the principles of justice, consultation, and accountability. Islamic teachings emphasize the importance of establishing a just and equitable system of governance, where leaders are chosen based on their competence, integrity, and commitment to serving the interests of the people.

One of the key teachings of Islam regarding governance is the concept of "Shura," or consultation. The Quran states, "And those who have responded to their lord and established prayer and whose affairs are [determined by] consultation among themselves, and from what We have provided them, they spend" (Quran 42:38). This verse highlights the importance of consulting with others and seeking their input in decision-making processes, emphasizing the importance of participatory governance in Islam.

Islam also emphasizes the importance of justice and fairness in governance. The Quran states, "Indeed, Allah commands justice, good conduct, and giving to relatives, and He forbids immorality, bad conduct, and oppression. He admonishes you that perhaps you will be reminded" (Quran 16:90). This verse highlights the importance of establishing a system of governance that upholds justice and fairness, ensuring that the rights of all individuals are protected and respected.

B: Rights and Responsibilities of Citizens in Islamic Societies

In Islamic societies, citizens have rights and responsibilities that are outlined in Islamic teachings. Citizens have the right to participate in the political process, to express their opinions and beliefs, and to hold their leaders accountable. At the same time, citizens have the responsibility to obey the laws of the land, to respect the rights of others, and to contribute to the well-being of society.

The Prophet Muhammad emphasized the importance of good governance and leadership, stating, "The best of your rulers are those whom you love and who love you, who pray for you and you pray for them. The worst of your rulers are those whom you hate and who hate you, whom you curse and who curse you" (Sahih Muslim). This Hadith highlights the importance of having leaders who are just, compassionate, and accountable to the people.

Overall, Islam emphasizes the importance of good governance, leadership, and political participation, highlighting the rights and responsibilities of citizens in Islamic societies. By upholding these principles, Muslims contribute to the establishment of a just and equitable society, where the rights of all individuals are protected and respected.

Chapter 18: Economic Rights

A: Islamic Principles of Economic Justice and Fair Trade

Islam emphasizes economic justice and fair trade, promoting principles of equity, compassion, and fairness in economic transactions. Islamic teachings provide guidance on economic matters, emphasizing the importance of wealth distribution, charity, and ethical business practices.

One of the key principles of Islamic economics is the concept of "Zakat," or obligatory charity. Zakat is a form of wealth redistribution that requires Muslims to give a portion of their wealth to those in need, including the poor, needy, and disadvantaged. The Quran states, "And establish prayer and give zakat, and whatever good you put forward for yourselves - you will find it with Allah. Indeed, Allah of what you do, is Seeing" (Quran 2:110). This verse highlights the importance of zakat as a means of purifying wealth and ensuring that it is distributed equitably among all members of society.

Islam also emphasizes the importance of fair trade and ethical business practices. The Prophet Muhammad said, "The seller and the buyer have the right to keep or return goods as long as they have not parted or till they part; and if both the parties spoke the truth and described the defects and qualities (of the goods), then they would be blessed in their transaction, and if they told lies or hid something, then the blessings of their transaction would be lost" (Sahih Bukhari). This Hadith emphasizes the importance of honesty, transparency, and fair dealing in business transactions, highlighting the importance of ethical conduct in Islamic economics.

B: Role of Business Ethics in Islamic Economics

In Islamic economics, business ethics play a crucial role in ensuring that economic activities are conducted in a manner that is ethical and in accordance with Islamic principles. Islamic teachings emphasize the importance of honesty, integrity, and fairness in business dealings, highlighting the value of ethical conduct in economic activities.

One of the key principles of business ethics in Islam is the concept of "Adl," or justice. The Quran states, "And do not consume one another's wealth unjustly or send it [in bribery] to the rulers in order that [they might aid] you [to] consume a portion of the wealth of the people in sin, while you know [it is unlawful]" (Quran 2:188). This verse highlights the prohibition of corruption and unjust enrichment in economic transactions, emphasizing the importance of conducting business in a fair and equitable manner.

Overall, Islam emphasizes the importance of economic justice, fair trade, and ethical business practices. By upholding these principles, Muslims contribute to the establishment of a just and equitable economic system, where the rights of all individuals are protected and respected.

Chapter 19: Health and Well-being

A: Islamic Teachings on Healthcare and Well-being

Islam places a strong emphasis on the importance of healthcare and well-being, recognizing the body as a trust from Allah that must be cared for and maintained. Islamic teachings provide guidance on maintaining good health and seeking medical treatment when necessary.

One of the key teachings of Islam regarding healthcare is the concept of "Tibb al-Nabawi," or Prophetic Medicine. The Prophet Muhammad emphasized the importance of natural remedies and treatments, stating, "Make use of medical treatment, for Allah has not made a disease without appointing a remedy for it, with the exception of one disease, namely old age" (Sunan Abu Dawood). This Hadith highlights the importance of seeking medical treatment and using natural remedies to maintain good health.

Islam also emphasizes the importance of cleanliness and hygiene in maintaining good health. The Prophet Muhammad said, "Cleanliness is half of faith" (Sahih Muslim), highlighting the importance of cleanliness in Islam. Muslims are encouraged to maintain good personal hygiene, including regular bathing, washing hands before and after meals, and keeping their surroundings clean.

B: Importance of Physical and Mental Health in Islamic Ethics

In addition to physical health, Islam also emphasizes the importance of mental health and well-being. The Quran states, "And whoever is conscious of Allah, He will make for him a way out and will provide for him from where he does not expect. And whoever relies upon Allah - then He is sufficient for him. Indeed, Allah will accomplish His purpose. Allah has already set for everything a [decreed] extent" (Quran 65:2-3). This verse highlights the importance of relying on Allah for support and seeking His guidance in times of difficulty, emphasizing the importance of mental resilience and well-being in Islamic ethics.

Furthermore, Islam emphasizes the importance of moderation in all aspects of life, including diet, exercise, and rest. The Prophet Muhammad said, "The best of people are those who have the longest lives and best in conduct" (Sunan Ibn Majah), highlighting the importance of maintaining a balanced and healthy lifestyle.

Overall, Islam emphasizes the importance of healthcare and well-being, recognizing the body as a trust from Allah that must be cared for and maintained. By upholding these principles, Muslims contribute to the promotion of good health and well-being in society.

Chapter 20: Education Rights

A: Islamic Perspective on the Importance of Education

Islam places a strong emphasis on the importance of education, recognizing it as a fundamental right and a means of acquiring knowledge and understanding of the world. Islamic teachings encourage Muslims to seek knowledge and education throughout their lives, emphasizing the value of learning in Islam.

One of the key teachings of Islam regarding education is the concept of "Iqra," or Read. The first word revealed in the Quran was "Iqra," which means "Read." This emphasizes the importance of reading and seeking knowledge in Islam. The Quran states, "Read! In the name of your Lord who created" (Quran 96:1), highlighting the importance of seeking knowledge and education in Islam.

Islam also emphasizes the importance of education for both men and women. The Prophet Muhammad said, "Seeking knowledge is obligatory upon every Muslim" (Sunan Ibn Majah), emphasizing the importance of education for all members of society. Islamic teachings also encourage parents to educate their children and provide them with the tools they need to succeed in life.

B: Rights and Responsibilities Related to Education in Islamic Societies

In Islamic societies, education is considered a fundamental right of every individual. Muslims have the right to seek education and acquire knowledge, regardless of their gender, background, or social status. Islamic teachings emphasize the importance of providing education for all members of society, ensuring that everyone has access to knowledge and learning opportunities.

Furthermore, Islam emphasizes the responsibilities of individuals and society towards education. Parents are responsible for educating their children and providing them with a good upbringing. The Prophet Muhammad said, "Every one of you is a shepherd and is responsible for his flock. The leader of people is a guardian and is responsible for his subjects..." (Sahih Bukhari), highlighting the responsibility of parents and leaders to educate and guide those under their care.

Overall, Islam places a strong emphasis on the importance of education, recognizing it as a fundamental right and a means of acquiring knowledge and understanding of the world. By upholding these principles, Muslims contribute to the promotion of education and knowledge in society, ensuring that everyone has access to learning opportunities and the tools they need to succeed in life.

Chapter 21: Refugees and Migration

A: Islamic Teachings on Caring for Refugees and Migrants

Islam places a strong emphasis on caring for refugees and migrants, recognizing their vulnerability and the importance of providing them with support and assistance. Islamic teachings emphasize compassion, generosity, and hospitality towards those in need, including refugees and migrants.

One of the key teachings of Islam regarding refugees and migrants is the concept of "Hijrah," or migration. The Prophet Muhammad himself migrated from Mecca to Medina in search of religious freedom and peace, setting an example for Muslims to follow. The Quran states, "And whoever leaves his home as an emigrant to Allah and His Messenger and then death overtakes him - his reward has already become incumbent upon Allah" (Quran 4:100), highlighting the importance of supporting and assisting migrants in their time of need.

Islam also emphasizes the importance of providing for the basic needs of refugees and migrants, including food, shelter, and clothing. The Quran states, "And they give food in spite of love for it to the needy, the orphan, and the captive" (Quran 76:8), emphasizing the importance of feeding the hungry and providing for those in need, including refugees and migrants.

B: Examples of Refugee Assistance in Islamic History

Islamic history is replete with examples of refugee assistance and support. During the early days of Islam, the

Prophet Muhammad and his companions provided refuge and assistance to those fleeing persecution and oppression. The city of Medina, where the Prophet migrated, became a sanctuary for Muslims fleeing persecution in Mecca, highlighting the importance of providing refuge and assistance to those in need.

Furthermore, Islamic empires and societies throughout history have provided assistance to refugees and migrants. The Ottoman Empire, for example, established a system of charitable foundations (waqf) to provide for the needs of refugees and migrants, ensuring that they were cared for and supported in their time of need.

Overall, Islam emphasizes the importance of caring for refugees and migrants, recognizing their vulnerability and the importance of providing them with support and assistance. By upholding these principles, Muslims contribute to the promotion of compassion, generosity, and hospitality towards those in need, including refugees and migrants.

Chapter 22: Conflict Resolution

A: Islamic Methods of Conflict Resolution and Peacebuilding

Islam promotes peaceful conflict resolution and emphasizes the importance of resolving disputes through dialogue, mediation, and arbitration. Islamic teachings provide guidance on how to resolve conflicts in a peaceful and just manner, emphasizing the importance of maintaining good relations and avoiding violence.

One of the key methods of conflict resolution in Islam is the concept of "Sulh," or reconciliation. The Quran encourages Muslims to seek reconciliation and peace in all matters, stating, "If two factions among the believers should fight, then make settlement between the two. But if one of them oppresses the other, then fight against the one that oppresses until it returns to the ordinance of Allah. And if it returns, then make settlement between them in justice and act justly. Indeed, Allah loves those who act justly" (Quran 49:9). This verse highlights the importance of seeking reconciliation and peace in conflicts, emphasizing the value of justice and fairness in resolving disputes.

Islam also emphasizes the importance of forgiveness and mercy in conflict resolution. The Prophet Muhammad said, "Do not be people without minds of your own, saying that if others treat you well you will treat them well, and that if they do wrong you will do wrong to them. Instead, accustom yourselves to do good if people do good and not to do wrong (even) if they do evil" (Sunan Abu Dawood). This Hadith emphasizes the importance of responding to aggression with forgiveness and kindness, promoting peace and reconciliation in conflicts.

B: Importance of Peaceful Coexistence in Islamic Teachings

Islam emphasizes the importance of peaceful coexistence and good relations with others, regardless of their background or beliefs. The Quran states, "And do good; indeed, Allah loves the doers of good" (Quran 2:195), highlighting the importance of doing good and promoting peace and harmony in society.

Furthermore, Islam emphasizes the importance of respecting the rights of others and avoiding harm to them. The Prophet Muhammad said, "None of you truly believes until he wishes for his brother what he wishes for himself" (Sahih Bukhari), highlighting the importance of empathy and compassion towards others.

Overall, Islam promotes peaceful conflict resolution and emphasizes the importance of peaceful coexistence and good relations with others. By upholding these principles, Muslims contribute to the promotion of peace and harmony in society, ensuring that conflicts are resolved peacefully and justly.

Chapter 23: International Relations

A: Islamic Principles of Diplomacy and International Cooperation

Islam promotes principles of diplomacy and international cooperation based on justice, equality, and mutual respect. Islamic teachings emphasize the importance of maintaining good relations with other nations and promoting peace and harmony in international relations.

One of the key principles of Islamic diplomacy is the concept of "Sulh," or reconciliation. The Quran encourages Muslims to seek reconciliation and peace in all matters, stating, "If they incline to peace, then incline to it [also] and rely upon Allah. Indeed, it is He who is the Hearing, the Knowing" (Quran 8:61). This verse highlights the importance of seeking peaceful solutions to conflicts and promoting reconciliation in international relations.

Islam also emphasizes the importance of treaties and agreements in international relations. The Prophet Muhammad himself made treaties with various tribes and nations, emphasizing the importance of honoring agreements and upholding trust in diplomatic relations. The Quran states, "And fulfill the covenant of Allah when you have taken it, [O believers], and do not break oaths after their confirmation while you have made Allah, over you, a witness. Indeed, Allah knows what you do" (Quran 16:91), highlighting the importance of honoring agreements and commitments in international relations.

B: Role of Islamic Ethics in Shaping International Relations

Islamic ethics play a crucial role in shaping international relations, promoting principles of justice, compassion, and fairness in dealings with other nations. Islamic teachings emphasize the importance of treating others with respect and dignity, regardless of their background or beliefs.

One of the key principles of Islamic ethics in international relations is the concept of "Adl," or justice. The Quran states, "Indeed, Allah commands justice and good conduct and giving to relatives and forbids immorality and bad conduct and oppression. He admonishes you that perhaps you will be reminded" (Quran 16:90), highlighting the importance of justice and fairness in international dealings.

Furthermore, Islam emphasizes the importance of peaceful coexistence and cooperation among nations. The Quran states, "And cooperate in righteousness and piety, but do not cooperate in sin and aggression. And fear Allah; indeed, Allah is severe in penalty" (Quran 5:2), highlighting the importance of working together for the common good and avoiding actions that harm others.

Overall, Islam promotes principles of diplomacy and international cooperation based on justice, equality, and mutual respect. By upholding these principles, Muslims contribute to the promotion of peace and harmony in international relations, ensuring that interactions between nations are based on principles of ethics and morality.

Chapter 24: Humanitarian Aid and Charity

A: Islamic Teachings on Charity and Humanitarian Aid

Islam emphasizes the importance of charity and humanitarian aid, recognizing them as fundamental principles of the faith. Islamic teachings encourage Muslims to be compassionate and generous towards those in need, emphasizing the importance of sharing wealth and resources with others.

One of the key teachings of Islam regarding charity is the concept of "Zakat," or obligatory charity. Zakat is one of the five pillars of Islam and requires Muslims to give a portion of their wealth to those in need, including the poor, needy, and disadvantaged. The Quran states, "And establish prayer and give zakat, and whatever good you put forward for yourselves - you will find it with Allah. Indeed, Allah of what you do, is Seeing" (Quran 2:110). This verse highlights the importance of zakat as a means of purifying wealth and ensuring that it is distributed equitably among all members of society.

Islam also emphasizes the importance of voluntary charity, known as "Sadaqah." The Prophet Muhammad said, "Charity does not decrease wealth" (Sahih Muslim), highlighting the importance of giving freely and generously to those in need. Sadaqah can take many forms, including giving money, food, or other resources to those in need, and is considered a virtuous act in Islam.

B: Examples of Islamic Organizations Providing Aid to Those in Need

Islamic organizations around the world are actively involved in providing aid and assistance to those in need, both within Muslim-majority countries and in other parts of the world. These organizations work to alleviate poverty, provide humanitarian assistance, and support communities affected by conflict and natural disasters.

One example of an Islamic organization providing aid to those in need is Islamic Relief Worldwide. Islamic Relief is an international humanitarian organization that provides emergency relief, healthcare, education, and sustainable development programs to communities in need around the world. The organization is guided by Islamic principles of compassion, mercy, and justice, and works to empower individuals and communities to overcome poverty and suffering.

Another example is the Red Crescent Movement, which is the Islamic equivalent of the Red Cross. The Red Crescent provides humanitarian assistance and relief to communities affected by conflict and natural disasters, following the principles of humanity, impartiality, neutrality, independence, voluntary service, unity, and universality.

Overall, Islam emphasizes the importance of charity and humanitarian aid, recognizing them as fundamental principles of the faith. By upholding these principles, Muslims contribute to the promotion of compassion, generosity, and solidarity with those in need, ensuring that humanitarian aid reaches those who need it most.

Chapter 25: Ethics in Business and Commerce

A: Islamic Principles of Ethical Business Practices

Islam emphasizes the importance of ethical business practices, promoting principles of honesty, fairness, and integrity in all commercial dealings. Islamic teachings provide guidance on how to conduct business ethically, ensuring that transactions are fair, transparent, and free from deception.

One of the key principles of Islamic ethics in business is the concept of "Halal" and "Haram." Halal refers to actions and practices that are permissible in Islam, while Haram refers to actions and practices that are prohibited. Islamic teachings prohibit practices such as fraud, deceit, and exploitation in business dealings, emphasizing the importance of honesty and integrity in all transactions.

Islam also emphasizes the importance of fulfilling contractual obligations and honoring agreements. The Quran states, "O you who have believed, fulfill [all] contracts" (Quran 5:1), highlighting the importance of honoring agreements and commitments in business dealings. Islamic teachings also emphasize the importance of treating employees, customers, and business partners with respect and fairness, ensuring that their rights are protected and respected.

B: Importance of Honesty and Fairness in Islamic Economics

In Islamic economics, honesty and fairness are considered fundamental principles that govern all economic activities.

Islam prohibits practices such as fraud, deception, and exploitation, emphasizing the importance of honesty and fairness in all economic transactions.

The Prophet Muhammad emphasized the importance of honesty and integrity in business dealings, stating, "The truthful and trustworthy businessman will be in the company of the prophets, the truthful, the martyrs, and the righteous on the Day of Judgment" (Sunan Abu Dawood). This Hadith highlights the importance of honesty and integrity in business, emphasizing the rewards for those who conduct themselves ethically in their dealings.

Furthermore, Islamic teachings emphasize the importance of fair pricing and avoiding exploitation in business transactions. The Prophet Muhammad said, "The seller and the buyer have the right to keep or return goods as long as they have not parted or till they part; and if both the parties spoke the truth and described the defects and qualities (of the goods), then they would be blessed in their transaction, and if they told lies or hid something, then the blessings of their transaction would be lost" (Sahih Bukhari). This Hadith emphasizes the importance of transparency and honesty in pricing and business practices.

Overall, Islam promotes principles of honesty, fairness, and integrity in business and commerce, ensuring that economic activities are conducted ethically and in accordance with Islamic teachings. By upholding these principles, Muslims contribute to the promotion of a fair and just economic system, where the rights of all individuals are protected and respected.

Chapter 26: Cultural Rights

A: Islamic Teachings on Cultural Diversity and Tolerance

Islam promotes cultural diversity and tolerance, recognizing the value of different cultures and traditions. Islamic teachings emphasize the importance of respecting and honoring cultural differences, promoting harmony and understanding among people of different backgrounds.

One of the key teachings of Islam regarding cultural diversity is the concept of "Ummah," or community. The Quran states, "O mankind, indeed We have created you from male and female and made you peoples and tribes that you may know one another. Indeed, the most noble of you in the sight of Allah is the most righteous of you. Indeed, Allah is Knowing and Acquainted" (Quran 49:13). This verse highlights the importance of diversity in human society and emphasizes the value of knowing and understanding one another's cultures and traditions.

Islam also emphasizes the importance of tolerance and coexistence among people of different cultures and backgrounds. The Quran states, "There shall be no compulsion in [acceptance of] the religion. The right course has become clear from the wrong. So whoever disbelieves in Taghut and believes in Allah has grasped the most trustworthy handhold with no break in it. And Allah is Hearing and Knowing" (Quran 2:256). This verse emphasizes the freedom of religion and belief, promoting tolerance and acceptance of different faiths and cultures.

B: Importance of Preserving Cultural Heritage in Islamic Societies

In Islamic societies, there is a strong emphasis on preserving cultural heritage and traditions. Islamic teachings encourage Muslims to preserve and protect their cultural heritage, recognizing it as a valuable part of their identity and history.

The Prophet Muhammad emphasized the importance of preserving cultural heritage, stating, "Whoever does not show mercy to our young ones, or honor our elders, is not from us" (Sunan Ibn Majah). This Hadith highlights the importance of respecting and honoring the cultural heritage of one's community, including the young and the old.

Furthermore, Islamic teachings emphasize the importance of preserving cultural heritage for future generations. The Quran states, "And when your Lord proclaimed, 'If you are grateful, I will surely increase you [in favor]; but if you deny, indeed, My punishment is severe'" (Quran 14:7). This verse emphasizes the importance of gratitude for blessings, including cultural heritage, and the responsibility to preserve it for future generations.

Overall, Islam promotes cultural diversity, tolerance, and the preservation of cultural heritage, recognizing the value of different cultures and traditions. By upholding these principles, Muslims contribute to the promotion of harmony and understanding among people of different backgrounds, ensuring that cultural rights are respected and protected.

Chapter 27: Technology and Innovation

A: Islamic Perspective on Technology and Innovation

Islam encourages the use of technology and innovation for the betterment of society and the advancement of human civilization. Islamic teachings emphasize the importance of knowledge and intellect, encouraging Muslims to seek knowledge and use it to improve their lives and the lives of others.

One of the key teachings of Islam regarding technology and innovation is the concept of "Ijtihad," or independent reasoning. Islamic scholars are encouraged to use their intellect and reasoning to interpret Islamic teachings and apply them to new situations, including technological advancements. The Quran states, "And We have certainly honored the children of Adam and carried them on the land and sea and provided for them of the good things and preferred them over much of what We have created, with [definite] preference" (Quran 17:70), highlighting the importance of using intellect and knowledge to improve society.

Islam also emphasizes the importance of using technology for beneficial purposes and avoiding its misuse. The Prophet Muhammad said, "Verily, Allah loves that when any one of you does a job, he should do it perfectly" (Sunan Ibn Majah), highlighting the importance of using technology responsibly and ethically.

B: Ethical Considerations Related to Technological Advancements in Islam

In Islam, there are ethical considerations related to technological advancements, particularly in the areas of privacy, environmental impact, and social justice. Islamic teachings emphasize the importance of using technology in a way that respects the rights of others and promotes the well-being of society as a whole.

For example, Islam emphasizes the importance of protecting privacy and confidentiality in technological communications. The Quran states, "O you who have believed, avoid much [negative] assumption. Indeed, some assumption is sin. And do not spy or backbite each other. Would one of you like to eat the flesh of his brother when dead? You would detest it. And fear Allah; indeed, Allah is Accepting of repentance and Merciful" (Quran 49:12), highlighting the importance of respecting the privacy and dignity of others.

Furthermore, Islam emphasizes the importance of using technology in a way that is environmentally sustainable. The Prophet Muhammad said, "The world is sweet and green [alluring] and verily Allah is going to install you as successors upon it in order to see how you act" (Sahih Muslim), highlighting the importance of preserving the environment for future generations.

Overall, Islam encourages the use of technology and innovation for the betterment of society, emphasizing the importance of using intellect and knowledge to improve human civilization. By upholding these principles, Muslims contribute to the promotion of ethical and responsible use of technology, ensuring that its benefits are maximized while its harms are minimized.

Chapter 28: Animal Rights

A: Islamic Teachings on Animal Welfare and Rights

Islam places a strong emphasis on animal welfare and rights, recognizing animals as part of Allah's creation and emphasizing the importance of treating them with compassion and care. Islamic teachings provide guidance on how to treat animals humanely and prohibit cruelty and abuse towards them.

One of the key teachings of Islam regarding animal welfare is the concept of "Mizan," or balance. The Quran states, "And the heaven He raised and imposed the balance. That you not transgress within the balance. And establish weight in justice and do not make deficient the balance" (Quran 55:7-9), highlighting the importance of maintaining balance and harmony in all aspects of life, including the treatment of animals.

Islam also emphasizes the importance of using animals for beneficial purposes and avoiding their misuse. The Prophet Muhammad said, "Whoever kills a sparrow or anything bigger than that without a just cause, Allah will hold him accountable on the Day of Judgment" (Sunan Abu Dawood), highlighting the importance of respecting the sanctity of animal life.

B: Importance of Compassion Towards Animals in Islamic Ethics

In Islamic ethics, compassion towards animals is considered a virtuous trait and is encouraged in all aspects of life. The Prophet Muhammad emphasized the importance of showing kindness and compassion towards animals, stating, "Whoever is kind to the creatures of Allah, he is kind to himself" (Sahih Bukhari), highlighting the importance of treating animals with care and compassion.

Furthermore, Islam emphasizes the importance of using animals for beneficial purposes and avoiding their misuse. The Prophet Muhammad said, "Verily, Allah has prescribed ihsan (proficiency, perfection) in all things. So if you kill, kill well; and if you slaughter, slaughter well. Let each one of you sharpen his blade and let him spare suffering to the animal he slaughters" (Sahih Muslim), highlighting the importance of using animals for food and other purposes in a humane and respectful manner.

Overall, Islam emphasizes the importance of animal welfare and rights, recognizing animals as part of Allah's creation and emphasizing the importance of treating them with compassion and care. By upholding these principles, Muslims contribute to the promotion of ethical and compassionate treatment of animals, ensuring that their rights are respected and protected.

Chapter 29: Social Welfare and Safety Nets

A: Islamic Teachings on Social Welfare and Safety Nets

Islam places a strong emphasis on social welfare and the importance of caring for the less fortunate members of society. Islamic teachings encourage Muslims to show compassion and generosity towards those in need, emphasizing the importance of providing for the welfare of the community as a whole.

One of the key teachings of Islam regarding social welfare is the concept of "Zakat," or obligatory charity. Zakat is one of the five pillars of Islam and requires Muslims to give a portion of their wealth to those in need, including the poor, needy, and disadvantaged. The Quran states, "And establish prayer and give zakat, and whatever good you put forward for yourselves - you will find it with Allah. Indeed, Allah of what you do, is Seeing" (Quran 2:110). This verse highlights the importance of zakat as a means of purifying wealth and ensuring that it is distributed equitably among all members of society.

Islam also emphasizes the importance of providing for the welfare of the community as a whole. The Prophet Muhammad said, "The example of the believers in their affection, mercy, and compassion for each other is that of a body. When any limb aches, the whole body reacts with sleeplessness and fever" (Sahih Bukhari), highlighting the importance of caring for the welfare of all members of society.

B: Role of Community Support in Addressing Social Issues in Islamic Societies

In Islamic societies, community support plays a crucial role in addressing social issues and providing for the welfare of the less fortunate. Islamic teachings emphasize the importance of solidarity and mutual support among members of the community, encouraging Muslims to work together to address social issues and provide for the welfare of all members of society.

One example of community support in Islamic societies is the concept of "Sadaqah," or voluntary charity. Muslims are encouraged to give freely and generously to those in need, including the poor, needy, and disadvantaged. The Prophet Muhammad said, "Charity does not decrease wealth" (Sahih Muslim), highlighting the importance of giving freely and generously to those in need.

Overall, Islam emphasizes the importance of social welfare and community support, recognizing them as fundamental principles of the faith. By upholding these principles, Muslims contribute to the promotion of compassion, generosity, and solidarity in society, ensuring that the welfare of all members of society is protected and respected.

Chapter 30: The Future of Human Rights in Islam

A: Challenges and Opportunities for Human Rights in the Islamic World

The Islamic world faces several challenges and opportunities regarding human rights. Some challenges include political instability, authoritarian regimes, and interpretations of Islamic law that may not align with modern human rights standards. However, there are also opportunities for progress, including a growing awareness of human rights issues, advancements in education and technology, and the potential for reform within Islamic societies.

One of the key challenges for human rights in the Islamic world is the interpretation of Islamic law, or Sharia. Some interpretations of Sharia may conflict with modern human rights standards, particularly regarding issues such as women's rights, freedom of expression, and LGBT rights. Addressing these challenges requires a nuanced understanding of Islamic law and a commitment to promoting human rights within the framework of Islamic teachings.

Another challenge is the political and social context in many Islamic countries, where authoritarian regimes may restrict basic freedoms and rights. Addressing these challenges requires a commitment to democratic governance and the rule of law, as well as efforts to promote accountability and transparency in government.

B: Ways to Promote Human Rights Based on Islamic Teachings

Despite these challenges, there are several ways to promote human rights based on Islamic teachings. One approach is to emphasize the universal values shared by Islam and human rights, such as justice, equality, and compassion. By highlighting these values, it is possible to show that Islam and human rights are not incompatible, but rather complementary.

Another approach is to promote education and awareness about human rights within Islamic communities. This can help dispel misconceptions about human rights and Sharia, and promote a more nuanced understanding of how Islamic teachings can support human rights principles.

Additionally, Islamic scholars and leaders can play a crucial role in promoting human rights within the Islamic world. By emphasizing the importance of human rights in Islamic teachings and promoting a more progressive interpretation of Sharia, they can help create a more inclusive and rights-respecting society.

Overall, the future of human rights in the Islamic world depends on the willingness of Islamic societies to engage with human rights principles and promote a more progressive interpretation of Islamic teachings. By addressing the challenges and seizing the opportunities, it is possible to create a future where human rights are respected and protected for all.

Chapter 31: Case Studies

A: Case Studies of Human Rights Issues in Islamic Societies

1: Women's Rights: In many Islamic societies, women face challenges in accessing their rights, including issues related to education, employment, and legal rights. For example, in Saudi Arabia, women have long been restricted in their ability to drive and travel without male permission, although recent reforms have started to address some of these restrictions.

2: Freedom of Expression: Many Islamic societies face challenges related to freedom of expression, with restrictions on media freedom and freedom of speech. For example, in countries like Iran and Saudi Arabia, journalists and activists have been arrested and detained for expressing dissenting views.

3: Minority Rights: Religious and ethnic minorities in Islamic societies often face discrimination and persecution. For example, the Rohingya Muslim minority in Myanmar has faced violence and persecution, leading to a humanitarian crisis.

B: Lessons Learned and Best Practices for Addressing Human Rights Challenges

1: Education and Awareness: One of the key lessons is the importance of education and awareness-raising about human rights issues. By educating people about their rights, it is possible to empower them to advocate for change and challenge discriminatory practices.

2: Legal Reforms: Legal reforms are essential for addressing human rights challenges in Islamic societies. For example, reforms in Saudi Arabia have led to changes in laws related to women's rights, including allowing women to drive and travel without male permission.

3: Dialogue and Engagement: Engaging with religious leaders, scholars, and communities is essential for addressing human rights challenges in Islamic societies. By promoting a more progressive interpretation of Islamic teachings, it is possible to create a more inclusive and rights-respecting society.

Overall, these case studies highlight the importance of addressing human rights challenges in Islamic societies through a combination of legal reforms, education, and dialogue. By learning from these experiences and adopting best practices, it is possible to create a future where human rights are respected and protected for all.

Chapter 32: Comparative Perspectives

A: Comparison of Human Rights Principles in Islam with Other Religious and Secular Perspectives

1: Islam: In Islam, human rights are grounded in the belief that all human beings are created by Allah and are entitled to dignity, respect, and freedom. Islamic teachings emphasize the importance of justice, compassion, and equality, and promote the rights of individuals to life, liberty, and security.

2: Christianity: Christianity also emphasizes the dignity and worth of every human being, based on the belief that all people are created in the image of God. Christian teachings emphasize the importance of love, forgiveness, and compassion, and promote the rights of individuals to freedom of conscience and belief.

3: Judaism: Judaism teaches the importance of justice, righteousness, and compassion, and promotes the rights of individuals to dignity, respect, and freedom. Jewish teachings emphasize the importance of caring for the vulnerable and marginalized in society, and promote the rights of individuals to freedom of worship and belief.

4: Secular Perspectives: Secular perspectives on human rights are often grounded in the belief in the inherent dignity and worth of every human being, independent of religious beliefs. Secular human rights principles emphasize the importance of individual freedom, equality, and justice, and promote the rights of individuals to freedom of expression, association, and religion.

B: Similarities and Differences in Approaches to Human Rights

1: Similarities: All three religious perspectives and secular perspectives share a common commitment to the inherent dignity and worth of every human being, and promote the rights of individuals to freedom, equality, and justice. They also emphasize the importance of compassion, empathy, and respect for others.

2: Differences: One key difference is in the source of human rights principles. In religious perspectives, human rights are often grounded in divine teachings or moral principles, while in secular perspectives, human rights are often based on principles of reason, ethics, and social justice. Additionally, there may be differences in the interpretation and application of human rights principles, based on cultural, historical, and philosophical differences.

Overall, while there are differences in the approaches to human rights between religious and secular perspectives, there are also many commonalities. By recognizing and building on these commonalities, it is possible to promote a more inclusive and rights-respecting society for all.

Chapter 33: Human Rights Advocacy

A: Strategies for Advocating for Human Rights Based on Islamic Principles

1: Education and Awareness: One of the key strategies for advocating for human rights based on Islamic principles is education and awareness-raising. This involves educating people about their rights and responsibilities, as well as promoting a more progressive interpretation of Islamic teachings that align with human rights principles.

2: Engagement with Religious Leaders: Engaging with religious leaders and scholars is essential for advocating for human rights based on Islamic principles. By promoting a more progressive interpretation of Islamic teachings, it is possible to show that Islam and human rights are not incompatible, but rather complementary.

3: Legal Reforms: Legal reforms are essential for advocating for human rights in the Islamic world. This involves advocating for changes in laws and policies that may be discriminatory or oppressive, and promoting laws that protect and promote human rights for all individuals.

4: Coalition Building: Building coalitions with other human rights organizations and activists can strengthen advocacy efforts and amplify voices calling for human rights based on Islamic principles. By working together, activists can create a more unified and effective advocacy movement.

B: Role of Activists and Organizations in Promoting Human Rights in the Islamic World

1: Activists: Activists play a crucial role in promoting human rights in the Islamic world. They work to raise awareness about human rights issues, advocate for legal reforms, and hold governments and institutions accountable for human rights violations. Activists often face significant challenges, including threats, harassment, and persecution, but their efforts are essential for promoting human rights and social justice.

2: Organizations: Human rights organizations play a key role in promoting human rights in the Islamic world. These organizations work to document human rights violations, provide support to victims, and advocate for policy changes. They also work to educate the public about human rights issues and promote a culture of human rights within Islamic societies.

Overall, human rights advocacy based on Islamic principles requires a multi-faceted approach that includes education, engagement, legal reforms, and coalition building. By working together, activists and organizations can promote human rights and social justice in the Islamic world, ensuring that the rights and dignity of all individuals are respected and protected.

Chapter 34: Legal Frameworks

A: Overview of Legal Frameworks for Human Rights in Islamic Countries

1: Constitutional Provisions: Many Islamic countries have constitutional provisions that guarantee basic human rights, such as the right to life, liberty, and equality before the law. However, the implementation of these provisions may vary widely, and there may be gaps in protection for certain groups, such as women, minorities, and marginalized communities.

2: Sharia Law: In many Islamic countries, Sharia law plays a significant role in the legal system. Sharia law is based on Islamic principles and teachings, and its interpretation and application can vary widely among different countries and legal traditions. Sharia law may be used to govern personal status matters, such as marriage, divorce, and inheritance, as well as criminal law and other areas of law.

3: International Human Rights Treaties: Many Islamic countries are parties to international human rights treaties, such as the Universal Declaration of Human Rights and the International Covenant on Civil and Political Rights. These treaties require countries to protect and promote human rights, although the extent to which countries comply with these obligations may vary.

B: Challenges and Opportunities for Legal Reform to Protect Human Rights

1: Challenges: One of the key challenges for legal reform to protect human rights in Islamic countries is the interpretation and application of Sharia law. Some interpretations of Sharia law may conflict with international human rights standards, particularly regarding issues such as women's rights, freedom of expression, and LGBT rights. Addressing these challenges requires a careful balancing of Islamic principles and international human rights standards.

2: Opportunities: Despite these challenges, there are opportunities for legal reform to protect human rights in Islamic countries. For example, some countries have undertaken legal reforms to strengthen protections for women's rights, such as reforms to family law and inheritance laws. These reforms demonstrate that it is possible to reconcile Islamic principles with modern human rights standards through careful interpretation and implementation.

Overall, legal frameworks for human rights in Islamic countries are complex and varied, reflecting the diverse legal traditions and interpretations of Islam. By addressing challenges and seizing opportunities for legal reform, it is possible to create legal frameworks that protect and promote human rights for all individuals in Islamic countries.

Chapter 35: Education and Awareness

A: Importance of Education and Awareness in Promoting Human Rights in Islamic Societies

1: Empowerment: Education and awareness play a crucial role in empowering individuals to understand and assert their rights. By educating people about their rights and responsibilities, they can become active participants in promoting and protecting human rights in their communities.

2: Prevention: Education and awareness can help prevent human rights violations by promoting a culture of respect for human rights and tolerance. By educating people about the importance of human rights and the consequences of human rights abuses, it is possible to create a more rights-respecting society.

3: Promotion of Values: Education and awareness can promote values such as justice, equality, and compassion, which are fundamental to human rights. By instilling these values in individuals from a young age, it is possible to create a society that values and respects the rights of all its members.

B: Role of Schools, Media, and Religious Institutions in Raising Awareness

1: Schools: Schools play a crucial role in raising awareness about human rights among young people. By incorporating human rights education into the curriculum, schools can help students understand the importance of human rights and how they can promote and protect them in their communities.

2: Media: The media can also play a key role in raising awareness about human rights issues. By reporting on human rights abuses and promoting a culture of respect for human rights, the media can help educate the public and create pressure for change.

3: Religious Institutions: Religious institutions can also play a role in raising awareness about human rights, particularly in Islamic societies. By promoting a more progressive interpretation of Islamic teachings that align with human rights principles, religious leaders can help create a more rights-respecting society.

Overall, education and awareness are essential for promoting human rights in Islamic societies. By empowering individuals to understand and assert their rights, and by promoting a culture of respect for human rights, it is possible to create a more just and rights-respecting society for all.

Chapter 36: Grassroots Movements

A: Examples of Grassroots Movements Promoting Human Rights in Islamic Societies

1: The Arab Spring: The Arab Spring was a series of grassroots movements that swept across the Middle East and North Africa in the early 2010s, calling for political reform, democracy, and human rights. While the outcomes of the Arab Spring were mixed, it demonstrated the power of grassroots movements in mobilizing people for change.

2: Women's Rights Movements: Women's rights movements in Islamic societies have been instrumental in advocating for gender equality and women's rights. For example, the "One Million Signatures Campaign" in Iran aimed to collect one million signatures in support of changing discriminatory laws against women.

3: Youth Movements: Youth movements in Islamic societies have also played a role in promoting human rights. For example, the "Youth Movement for Justice" in Saudi Arabia has advocated for political reform and human rights.

B: Strategies for Building a Grassroots Movement for Human Rights

1: Building Networks: Building networks of like-minded individuals and organizations is crucial for building a grassroots movement for human rights. By connecting with others who share similar goals and values, it is possible to amplify voices and mobilize support for human rights causes.

2: Raising Awareness: Raising awareness about human rights issues is essential for building a grassroots movement. This can be done through education, advocacy campaigns, and media outreach to inform the public about human rights abuses and the need for change.

3: Mobilizing Support: Mobilizing support from the community is key to building a grassroots movement. This can be done through rallies, protests, petitions, and other forms of activism to show solidarity and demand change.

4: Engaging with Authorities: Engaging with authorities and policymakers is important for building a grassroots movement. By advocating for policy changes and reforms, grassroots movements can influence decision-making and bring about meaningful change.

Overall, grassroots movements play a crucial role in promoting human rights in Islamic societies. By mobilizing people, raising awareness, and advocating for change, grassroots movements can help create a more just and rights-respecting society for all.

Chapter 37: International Cooperation

A: Importance of International Cooperation in Promoting Human Rights

1: Global Challenges: Many human rights issues, such as poverty, conflict, and environmental degradation, are global in nature and require international cooperation to address effectively. By working together, countries can pool resources and expertise to tackle these challenges.

2: Normative Framework: International cooperation helps establish a normative framework for human rights, setting standards and guidelines for countries to follow. Through international agreements and treaties, countries commit to upholding human rights principles and can be held accountable for any violations.

3: Exchange of Best Practices: International cooperation allows for the exchange of best practices and experiences in promoting human rights. Countries can learn from each other's successes and failures, and adapt their approaches accordingly.

B: Role of Islamic Countries in Advancing Human Rights Globally

1: Support for International Agreements: Many Islamic countries are party to international human rights agreements and treaties, demonstrating their commitment to upholding human rights globally. By ratifying these agreements, Islamic countries pledge to adhere to international human rights standards.

2: Promotion of Islamic Values: Islamic countries can play a role in advancing human rights globally by promoting Islamic values that align with human rights principles, such as justice, equality, and compassion. By highlighting these values, Islamic countries can contribute to the promotion of human rights worldwide.

3: Participation in International Forums: Islamic countries can participate in international forums and organizations dedicated to human rights, such as the United Nations Human Rights Council. By engaging in these forums, Islamic countries can contribute to shaping global human rights policies and initiatives.

4: Humanitarian Assistance: Islamic countries can also contribute to advancing human rights globally through humanitarian assistance and aid. By providing support to countries and communities in need, Islamic countries can help alleviate suffering and promote human dignity.

Overall, international cooperation is essential for promoting human rights globally. Islamic countries can play a significant role in this effort by supporting international agreements, promoting Islamic values, participating in international forums, and providing humanitarian assistance. By working together, countries can create a more just and rights-respecting world for all.

Chapter 38: Challenges and Controversies

A: Challenges and Controversies Surrounding Human Rights in Islam

1: Interpretation of Sharia: One of the main challenges is the interpretation of Sharia law, which can vary widely among different scholars and traditions. Some interpretations may be seen as incompatible with modern human rights standards, particularly regarding issues such as women's rights, freedom of expression, and LGBT rights.

2: Cultural and Societal Norms: Cultural and societal norms in Islamic societies can also present challenges to human rights. Some cultural practices may be at odds with human rights principles, such as the practice of child marriage or female genital mutilation.

3: Political Instability: Political instability in many Islamic countries can hinder efforts to promote and protect human rights. Authoritarian regimes may restrict basic freedoms and rights, leading to human rights violations.

4: Misconceptions and Stereotypes: There are often misconceptions and stereotypes about Islam and human rights, which can fuel discrimination and prejudice. These misconceptions can hinder efforts to promote human rights in Islamic societies.

B: Strategies for Addressing Misconceptions and Challenges

1: Education and Awareness: Education and awareness-raising are key strategies for addressing misconceptions and challenges surrounding human rights in Islam. By educating people about human rights principles and how they align with Islamic teachings, it is possible to dispel misconceptions and promote a more nuanced understanding of the issue.

2: Dialogue and Engagement: Dialogue and engagement with religious leaders, scholars, and communities are essential for addressing challenges surrounding human rights in Islam. By promoting a more progressive interpretation of Islamic teachings, it is possible to show that Islam and human rights are not incompatible, but rather complementary.

3: Legal Reforms: Legal reforms are crucial for addressing human rights challenges in Islamic societies. By advocating for changes in laws and policies that may be discriminatory or oppressive, it is possible to create a legal framework that protects and promotes human rights for all individuals.

4: International Cooperation: International cooperation is also important for addressing human rights challenges in Islamic societies. By working together with other countries and organizations, Islamic countries can share best practices and experiences in promoting human rights, and can work together to address global challenges.

Overall, addressing challenges and misconceptions surrounding human rights in Islam requires a multi-faceted approach that includes education, dialogue, legal reforms, and international cooperation. By addressing these challenges, it is possible to create a more just and rights-respecting society for all.

Chapter 39: Human Rights and Development

A: Relationship Between Human Rights and Development in Islamic Societies

1: Empowerment: Human rights are closely linked to development in Islamic societies, as they empower individuals to participate fully in the development process. By ensuring that individuals have access to education, healthcare, and opportunities for economic advancement, human rights contribute to overall development in Islamic societies.

2: Inclusivity: Human rights promote inclusivity in development, ensuring that all members of society, including women, minorities, and marginalized communities, have equal access to development opportunities. This inclusivity is essential for sustainable and equitable development in Islamic societies.

3: Accountability: Human rights also play a role in promoting accountability in development. By holding governments and institutions accountable for their actions and policies, human rights help ensure that development efforts are transparent, accountable, and effective.

B: Role of Human Rights in Promoting Sustainable Development

1: Social Justice: Human rights promote social justice, which is essential for sustainable development. By ensuring that all members of society have access to basic rights and opportunities, human rights contribute to a more equitable and just society, which is essential for long-term development.

2: Environmental Protection: Human rights also play a role in promoting environmental protection, which is crucial for sustainable development. By recognizing the right to a healthy environment, human rights help ensure that development is sustainable and does not harm the environment or future generations.

3: Good Governance: Human rights are closely linked to good governance, which is essential for sustainable development. By promoting transparency, accountability, and the rule of law, human rights help ensure that development efforts are effective and sustainable.

Overall, human rights are essential for development in Islamic societies, as they promote empowerment, inclusivity, and accountability. By promoting human rights, Islamic societies can achieve sustainable development that benefits all members of society.

Chapter 40: Gender Equality

A: Progress and Challenges in Achieving Gender Equality in Islamic Societies

1: Progress: There has been significant progress in recent years towards achieving gender equality in Islamic societies. Many countries have implemented legal reforms to improve women's rights, such as laws promoting gender equality in education, employment, and political participation.

2: Challenges: Despite progress, there are still many challenges to achieving gender equality in Islamic societies. These challenges include cultural norms and practices that discriminate against women, as well as legal and institutional barriers that limit women's rights and opportunities.

3: Intersectionality: Gender equality in Islamic societies is also influenced by factors such as class, ethnicity, and religion. Intersectionality plays a role in shaping women's experiences and opportunities, and must be taken into account in efforts to promote gender equality.

B: Strategies for Promoting Gender Equality Based on Islamic Teachings

1: Education and Awareness: Education and awareness-raising are key strategies for promoting gender equality based on Islamic teachings. By educating people about the rights of women in Islam and challenging misconceptions, it is possible to promote a more progressive understanding of gender equality.

2: Legal Reforms: Legal reforms are crucial for promoting gender equality in Islamic societies. By advocating for changes in laws that discriminate against women and promote gender equality, it is possible to create a legal framework that protects and promotes women's rights.

3: Empowerment: Empowering women to participate fully in society is essential for promoting gender equality. This includes ensuring that women have access to education, healthcare, and economic opportunities, as well as promoting women's participation in decision-making processes.

4: Engagement with Religious Leaders: Engaging with religious leaders and scholars is important for promoting gender equality based on Islamic teachings. By promoting a more progressive interpretation of Islamic teachings that align with gender equality principles, religious leaders can help create a more inclusive and rights-respecting society.

Overall, achieving gender equality in Islamic societies requires a multi-faceted approach that includes legal reforms, education, empowerment, and engagement with religious leaders. By addressing these challenges and promoting gender equality based on Islamic teachings, it is possible to create a more just and equitable society for all.

Chapter 41: Youth and Human Rights

A: Role of Youth in Promoting Human Rights in Islamic Societies

1: Agents of Change: Youth are often at the forefront of promoting human rights in Islamic societies. They bring fresh perspectives, energy, and innovation to human rights advocacy, and are instrumental in driving social and political change.

2: Education and Awareness: Youth are key agents in raising awareness about human rights issues in Islamic societies. Through education and advocacy, they can help educate their peers and communities about human rights principles and the importance of respecting human dignity.

3: Advocacy and Activism: Youth play a crucial role in advocating for human rights reforms in Islamic societies. They participate in protests, campaigns, and other forms of activism to raise awareness and demand change from their governments and institutions.

B: Strategies for Engaging Youth in Human Rights Advocacy

1: Education and Training: Providing youth with education and training in human rights principles and advocacy strategies is essential for engaging them in human rights advocacy. This can be done through workshops, seminars, and educational programs that empower youth to become effective advocates for human rights.

2: Youth-led Initiatives: Supporting youth-led initiatives and organizations is important for engaging youth in human rights advocacy. By providing resources, mentorship, and guidance, it is possible to empower youth to take ownership of human rights issues and drive change in their communities.

3: Digital and Social Media: Utilizing digital and social media platforms is an effective strategy for engaging youth in human rights advocacy. Platforms such as Facebook, Twitter, and Instagram can be used to raise awareness, mobilize support, and amplify youth voices on human rights issues.

4: Partnerships and Networks: Building partnerships and networks with youth organizations, schools, and community groups is essential for engaging youth in human rights advocacy. By working together, it is possible to create a more coordinated and impactful advocacy movement.

Overall, engaging youth in human rights advocacy is crucial for promoting human rights in Islamic societies. By recognizing the important role that youth play and implementing strategies to engage them effectively, it is possible to create a more just and rights-respecting society for all.

Chapter 42: Media and Communication

A: Role of Media and Communication in Promoting Human Rights

1: Information Dissemination: Media and communication channels play a crucial role in disseminating information about human rights issues in Islamic societies. They help raise awareness about violations, advocate for justice, and empower individuals to take action.

2: Public Awareness: Media can help create public awareness about human rights principles and values. Through news reporting, documentaries, and other forms of media, people can learn about their rights and the importance of respecting the rights of others.

3: Advocacy and Activism: Media can serve as a platform for advocacy and activism on human rights issues. By highlighting stories of injustice, media can mobilize public support for change and hold governments and institutions accountable for their actions.

B: Importance of Responsible Journalism in Islamic Societies

1: Ethical Reporting: Responsible journalism is essential for promoting human rights in Islamic societies. Journalists have a duty to report accurately and ethically on human rights issues, ensuring that they do not perpetuate stereotypes or misinformation that could harm individuals or communities.

2: Balanced Coverage: Balanced coverage of human rights issues is important in Islamic societies. Journalists should strive to present a balanced perspective that reflects the complexity of human rights issues and the diverse viewpoints of those affected.

3: Respect for Diversity: Journalists should respect the diversity of Islamic societies and avoid stereotyping or stigmatizing any group based on religion, ethnicity, or gender. Responsible journalism promotes understanding and tolerance, which are essential for promoting human rights.

4: Accountability: Journalists should hold themselves accountable for their reporting and strive to correct any inaccuracies or biases in their coverage. By upholding high standards of journalism, media can contribute to a more informed and rights-respecting society.

Overall, media and communication play a crucial role in promoting human rights in Islamic societies. By providing accurate information, raising public awareness, and advocating for justice, media can help create a more just and rights-respecting society for all.

Chapter 43: Religious Freedom

A: Islamic Perspective on Religious Freedom and Tolerance

1: Quranic Teachings: The Quran emphasizes the importance of religious freedom and tolerance. Surah Al-Baqarah (2:256) states, "There is no compulsion in religion," highlighting the principle that individuals should be free to choose and practice their religion without coercion.

2: Prophetic Traditions: The teachings and actions of the Prophet Muhammad also emphasize religious freedom and tolerance. The Prophet's Constitution of Medina, for example, granted religious freedom to all residents of Medina, regardless of their faith.

3: Historical Examples: Throughout Islamic history, there are many examples of religious tolerance and coexistence. Islamic societies have often welcomed and protected religious minorities, allowing them to practice their faith freely.

B: Challenges and Opportunities for Religious Freedom in Islamic Societies

1: Extremism and Intolerance: One of the main challenges to religious freedom in Islamic societies is extremism and intolerance. Some interpretations of Islam promote exclusivist views that do not tolerate religious diversity, leading to discrimination and persecution of religious minorities.

2: Legal and Political Restrictions: In some Islamic societies, there are legal and political restrictions on religious freedom. Blasphemy laws, for example, can be used to restrict the freedom of expression and religion of individuals who hold dissenting views.

3: Opportunities for Reform: Despite challenges, there are also opportunities for reform to promote religious freedom in Islamic societies. By promoting a more progressive interpretation of Islamic teachings that emphasizes tolerance and pluralism, it is possible to create a more inclusive and rights-respecting society.

4: Interfaith Dialogue: Interfaith dialogue and engagement can also promote religious freedom in Islamic societies. By fostering understanding and respect between different religious communities, it is possible to create a more harmonious and tolerant society.

Overall, religious freedom is a fundamental human right that is rooted in Islamic teachings. By addressing challenges and promoting a more inclusive interpretation of Islam, it is possible to create a more tolerant and rights-respecting society for all.

Chapter 44: Accountability and Justice

A: Importance of Accountability and Justice in Protecting Human Rights

1: Deterrent Effect: Accountability and justice serve as deterrents to human rights violations. Knowing that there are consequences for their actions can deter individuals and institutions from committing human rights abuses.

2: Restoration of Dignity: Accountability and justice help restore the dignity of victims of human rights violations. By holding perpetrators accountable, victims can receive acknowledgment of their suffering and a sense of justice being served.

3: Prevention of Recurrence: Accountability and justice help prevent the recurrence of human rights violations. By addressing the root causes of violations and implementing measures to prevent future abuses, accountability mechanisms contribute to long-term protection of human rights.

B: Role of Accountability Mechanisms in Ensuring Human Rights are Upheld

1: Legal Mechanisms: Legal mechanisms, such as courts and tribunals, play a crucial role in holding perpetrators of human rights violations accountable. These mechanisms provide a formal process for seeking justice and can lead to prosecutions and convictions of perpetrators.

2: Truth and Reconciliation Commissions: Truth and reconciliation commissions are another accountability mechanism that can help address human rights violations.

These commissions provide a platform for victims to share their experiences, and for perpetrators to confess their crimes, leading to a more comprehensive understanding of past abuses.

3: International Tribunals: International tribunals, such as the International Criminal Court (ICC), play a role in ensuring accountability for serious human rights violations that fall under their jurisdiction. These tribunals can prosecute individuals responsible for genocide, war crimes, and crimes against humanity.

4: Civil Society Monitoring: Civil society plays a crucial role in monitoring and documenting human rights violations. Through reports, advocacy, and campaigns, civil society organizations can raise awareness about violations and pressure governments and institutions to take action.

5: Transitional Justice: Transitional justice mechanisms, such as reparations and institutional reforms, are important for ensuring accountability and justice in post-conflict or transitional societies. These mechanisms help address the legacy of past abuses and promote reconciliation and peace.

Overall, accountability and justice are essential for protecting human rights. By holding perpetrators accountable and addressing the root causes of violations, accountability mechanisms play a crucial role in ensuring that human rights are upheld and respected for all.

Chapter 45: Peacebuilding and Reconciliation

A: Islamic Teachings on Peacebuilding and Reconciliation

1: Concept of Peace: Islam emphasizes the importance of peace as a fundamental value. The Quran promotes peace as a state of harmony and tranquility that is achievable through submission to the will of God and the pursuit of justice.

2: Forgiveness and Reconciliation: Islamic teachings encourage forgiveness and reconciliation as ways to resolve conflicts and restore relationships. The Prophet Muhammad is known for his teachings on forgiveness and his ability to reconcile warring tribes.

3: Conflict Resolution: Islam provides guidance on resolving conflicts through peaceful means. The Quran encourages dialogue and negotiation to resolve disputes, and prohibits aggression and violence except in self-defense.

B: Strategies for Promoting Peace and Reconciliation in Islamic Societies

1: Education and Awareness: Promoting education and awareness about Islamic teachings on peace and reconciliation is crucial. By educating people about these principles, it is possible to promote a culture of peace and tolerance in Islamic societies.

2: Interfaith Dialogue: Engaging in interfaith dialogue is important for promoting peace and reconciliation in Islamic societies. By fostering understanding and respect between different religious communities, it is possible to reduce tensions and promote peaceful coexistence.

3: Conflict Resolution Mechanisms: Establishing effective conflict resolution mechanisms is essential for promoting peace and reconciliation. These mechanisms should be accessible, impartial, and based on principles of justice and fairness.

4: Community Engagement: Engaging communities in peacebuilding and reconciliation efforts is important. By involving local communities in decision-making processes and empowering them to resolve conflicts peacefully, it is possible to build sustainable peace.

5: Leadership and Governance: Effective leadership and good governance are essential for promoting peace and reconciliation. Leaders should promote a culture of peace, tolerance, and inclusivity, and should work towards addressing the root causes of conflict.

Overall, promoting peace and reconciliation in Islamic societies requires a multi-faceted approach that includes education, dialogue, conflict resolution mechanisms, community engagement, and effective leadership. By implementing these strategies, it is possible to build a more peaceful and harmonious society based on Islamic principles.

Chapter 46: Ethics of War

A: Islamic Principles Related to the Conduct of War

1: Just War Theory: Islam, like many other religions, has a concept of a "just war," which is a war that is fought for a righteous cause and in a just manner. Islamic teachings emphasize the importance of fighting only in self-defense or to protect the innocent.

2: Prohibition of Aggression: Islam prohibits aggression and the use of force except in self-defense. The Quran states, "Fight in the way of Allah those who fight you but do not transgress. Indeed, Allah does not like transgressors" (Surah Al-Baqarah, 2:190).

3: Protection of Non-Combatants: Islamic teachings emphasize the protection of non-combatants, including civilians, women, children, and the elderly, during times of war. The Prophet Muhammad forbade the killing of non-combatants and the destruction of property.

4: Ethical Conduct: Islamic teachings emphasize the importance of ethical conduct in war. Soldiers are encouraged to show mercy and compassion to their enemies, and to avoid unnecessary harm and destruction.

B: Importance of Ethical Considerations in Times of Conflict

1: Human Dignity: Ethical considerations in times of conflict are important for upholding the dignity of all individuals, including combatants and non-combatants. Treating others with respect and compassion, even in war, is a fundamental principle of Islam.

2: Prevention of Atrocities: Ethical considerations help prevent atrocities and human rights abuses in times of conflict. By adhering to ethical principles, it is possible to minimize the suffering and harm caused by war.

3: International Law: Ethical considerations in war are also important for ensuring compliance with international humanitarian law, which sets out rules for the conduct of armed conflict. Adhering to these rules helps protect civilians and minimize the impact of war on communities.

4: Long-Term Peace: Ethical conduct in times of conflict contributes to long-term peace and reconciliation. By treating adversaries with respect and compassion, it is possible to build trust and lay the groundwork for peaceful coexistence in the future.

In conclusion, ethical considerations in times of conflict are essential for upholding human dignity, preventing atrocities, ensuring compliance with international law, and promoting long-term peace. By adhering to ethical principles, it is possible to mitigate the impact of war and build a more just and peaceful world.

Chapter 47: Governance and Human Rights

A: Relationship Between Governance and Human Rights in Islamic Societies

1: Islamic Principles of Governance: Islam provides principles of governance that emphasize justice, accountability, and the protection of human rights. The Quran and the teachings of the Prophet Muhammad emphasize the importance of good governance and the rights of individuals.

2: Shura (Consultation): Shura is a principle of governance in Islam that emphasizes consultation and participation in decision-making. This principle promotes transparency, accountability, and inclusivity in governance, which are essential for protecting human rights.

3: Rule of Law: Islamic teachings emphasize the importance of the rule of law in governance. The Quran states, "O you who have believed, obey Allah and obey the Messenger and those in authority among you" (Surah An-Nisa, 4:59), highlighting the importance of following the law and respecting authority.

B: Role of Good Governance in Protecting Human Rights

1: Protection of Rights: Good governance plays a crucial role in protecting human rights. By ensuring that laws and policies are in place to protect the rights of individuals, governments can create a framework for respecting and promoting human rights.

2: Accountability: Good governance promotes accountability, which is essential for protecting human rights. Governments that are accountable to their citizens are more likely to respect human rights and address violations effectively.

3: Transparency: Transparency in governance is important for protecting human rights. By ensuring that government actions are transparent and open to scrutiny, it is possible to prevent abuses of power and promote accountability.

4: Participation: Good governance promotes participation and engagement of all members of society in decision-making processes. By ensuring that all voices are heard, governments can create policies that respect and promote human rights.

Overall, the relationship between governance and human rights in Islamic societies is based on principles of justice, accountability, and the rule of law. By promoting good governance, Islamic societies can protect and promote human rights for all individuals.

Chapter 48: Legal Protections

A: Legal Protections for Human Rights in Islamic Law

1: Islamic Law (Sharia): Islamic law, or Sharia, provides a framework for legal protections for human rights in Islamic societies. Sharia emphasizes justice, equality, and the protection of individual rights.

2: Constitutional Provisions: Many Islamic countries have constitutional provisions that protect human rights. These provisions often include guarantees of freedom of religion, expression, and association, as well as protections against discrimination.

3: International Human Rights Treaties: Islamic countries are also party to international human rights treaties that provide legal protections for human rights. These treaties include the Universal Declaration of Human Rights and the International Covenant on Civil and Political Rights.

4: Islamic Jurisprudence: Islamic jurisprudence, or fiqh, provides interpretations of Islamic law that can be used to protect human rights. Islamic jurists have developed principles and guidelines for protecting the rights of individuals in accordance with Islamic teachings.

B: Challenges and Opportunities for Strengthening Legal Protections

1: Interpretation of Sharia: One challenge is the interpretation of Sharia in a way that is consistent with modern human rights standards. There is a need to reconcile traditional interpretations of Sharia with contemporary understandings of human rights.

2: Implementation of Laws: Another challenge is the implementation of laws and regulations that protect human rights. In some Islamic societies, there may be a gap between the law and its implementation, leading to violations of human rights.

3: Cultural and Religious Norms: Cultural and religious norms can also pose challenges to legal protections for human rights. In some cases, these norms may conflict with human rights principles, making it difficult to fully protect human rights.

4: Capacity Building: One opportunity for strengthening legal protections is capacity building. By training judges, lawyers, and other legal professionals on human rights principles, it is possible to improve the implementation of laws that protect human rights.

5: Dialogue and Engagement: Dialogue and engagement with religious scholars and leaders are also important for strengthening legal protections for human rights. By promoting a more progressive understanding of Islamic teachings, it is possible to align Sharia with modern human rights standards.

Overall, legal protections for human rights in Islamic societies are based on Islamic law, constitutional provisions, and international treaties. By addressing challenges and seizing opportunities, it is possible to strengthen these legal protections and ensure that human rights are protected for all individuals.

Chapter 49: Social Movements and Change

A: Strategies for Mobilizing Communities for Social Change

1: Education and Awareness: Educating communities about social issues and the need for change is crucial for mobilizing them. This can be done through workshops, seminars, and campaigns that raise awareness and promote understanding of the issues.

2: Organizing and Networking: Organizing communities and building networks of like-minded individuals and organizations is important for mobilizing collective action. By working together, communities can amplify their voices and increase their impact.

3: Advocacy and Campaigning: Advocacy and campaigning are effective strategies for mobilizing communities for social change. This can involve lobbying policymakers, organizing protests and demonstrations, and using social media to raise awareness and mobilize support.

4: Coalition Building: Building coalitions with other social movements and organizations can strengthen efforts for social change. By joining forces with others who share similar goals, communities can increase their influence and effectiveness.

5: Community Engagement: Engaging community members in decision-making processes and empowering them to take action is essential for mobilizing communities for social change. By involving community members in planning and implementing initiatives, it is possible to build a sense of ownership and commitment to the cause.

B: Examples of Successful Social Movements in Islamic History

1: The Abolition of Slavery: Islamic history includes examples of successful social movements that have led to significant change. One such example is the abolition of slavery, which was achieved through the efforts of abolitionist movements that campaigned for the end of slavery based on Islamic teachings of justice and equality.

2: Women's Rights: Another example is the women's rights movement in Islamic history, which has led to improvements in the status and rights of women. Women's rights activists have campaigned for changes in laws and social norms to ensure that women are treated fairly and equally.

3: Civil Rights: Islamic history also includes examples of movements for civil rights, including movements that have advocated for the rights of minorities and marginalized communities. These movements have worked to ensure that all individuals are treated with dignity and respect, regardless of their background or beliefs.

4: Environmental Conservation: In recent years, there has been a growing movement for environmental conservation in Islamic societies. This movement has been driven by Islamic teachings on the importance of protecting the environment and has led to initiatives to promote sustainable living and conservation efforts.

Overall, social movements in Islamic history have been instrumental in driving social change and promoting justice, equality, and human rights. By learning from these examples and employing effective strategies for mobilizing communities, it is possible to continue to drive positive change in Islamic societies today.

Chapter 50: Conclusion

A: Recap of Key Concepts and Principles Discussed in the Book

Throughout this book, we have explored the relationship between Islam and human rights, examining key concepts, principles, and teachings that guide the protection and promotion of human rights in Islamic societies. Some of the key concepts and principles discussed include:

1: Islamic Teachings: Islam emphasizes the importance of justice, compassion, and equality, which form the foundation of human rights in Islamic teachings.

2: Legal Protections: Islamic law provides a framework for protecting human rights, including constitutional provisions and international treaties that uphold human rights principles.

3: Ethical Considerations: Islamic ethics emphasize the importance of ethical conduct in times of conflict and the protection of human dignity.

4: Governance: Good governance plays a crucial role in protecting human rights, ensuring accountability, and promoting justice.

5: Social Movements: Social movements have historically played a significant role in promoting social change and advancing human rights in Islamic societies.

B: Call to Action for Promoting Human Rights Based on Islamic Teachings

As we conclude this book, it is important to recognize the role that each individual can play in promoting human rights based on Islamic teachings. We are called upon to:

1: Educate Ourselves and Others: Educate ourselves and others about human rights principles and how they are rooted in Islamic teachings.

2: Advocate for Change: Advocate for change within our communities and societies to ensure that human rights are protected and respected for all individuals.

3: Engage in Dialogue: Engage in dialogue with others, including religious scholars, leaders, and policymakers, to promote a more inclusive and rights-respecting society.

4: Support Social Movements: Support social movements and organizations that are working to promote human rights based on Islamic teachings.

5: Lead by Example: Lead by example in our own lives, demonstrating compassion, justice, and equality in our interactions with others.

By following these principles and taking action in our own lives, we can contribute to the promotion and protection of human rights in Islamic societies and beyond, ensuring a more just and rights-respecting world for all.

About the author Binish Shah

Binish Shah Expertise in sales management extends globally, where she crafts strategic approaches for various international companies. Her role involves devising tailored strategies for companies traversing the globe, leveraging her extensive sales experience and understanding of diverse markets.

Beyond her professional prowess, Binish Shah passion for personal development shines. She embraces mindfulness, honing its practical applications for enhanced focus and mental well-being. Her journey includes conquering stage fright, mastering public speaking, and fostering personal growth.

Financially astute, Binish Shah adeptly manages personal finances, drawing on her understanding of influence and persuasion across both professional and personal spheres.

Despite a busy schedule, maintaining a healthy lifestyle remains paramount to Binish Shah. She not only creates nutritious meals swiftly but also explores meditation practices for inner tranquility.

Emphasizing healthy relationships through effective communication and boundaries, Binish Shah values continual self-reflection and personal growth.

Networking stands as a cornerstone for her career advancement. She refines time management skills to maximize productivity and attain her objectives.

Her grasp of investment fundamentals enables informed financial decisions. To maintain equilibrium, Binish Shah delves into stress reduction techniques like mindfulness, yoga, and meditation, fostering a balanced mindset.

Yours Sincerely

Binish Shah

Email: binish728@gmail.com

www.ingramcontent.com/pod-product-compliance
Lightning Source LLC
Chambersburg PA
CBHW071041250726
48653CB00005B/1945